Cuba Under Embargo

The Macro Impact

Joe Atikian

Copyright © 2012 by Joe Atikian

All rights reserved. No part of this book may be reproduced in any form or by any means, mechanical or electronic or other, including photocopying, recording or by any information storage or retrieval system, without the prior written permission of the author except for brief quotations for use in reviews or articles.

Cover design by Joe Atikian

Cuba Under Embargo: The Macro Impact
2nd Edition

ISBN-13: 978-1477445914
ISBN-10: 1477445919

Also available as an e-book at most online retailers.

For updates and more information visit the author's website, www.atikian.com

Other books by Joe Atikian

Saving Money: The Missing Link

Industrial Shift:
The Structure of the New World Economy

Table of Contents

1 Introduction 1

2 The Data Problem 17

3 Cuba's Unlikely Growth 25

4 Comparing Regional Growth 41

5 The Global Trade Surprise 55

6 Revealing Industrial Structure 85

7 Human Development in Cuba 107

8 The Macro Impact 119

Appendix 1: Embargo Timeline 124

Appendix 2: Web Link Resources 128

Appendix 3: Reading List 131

Appendix 4: Glossary 136

Castro, Guevara, et al. Havana May 5, 1960
Source: Museo Che Guevara, Havana (public domain)

Col. Batista, Gen. Malin Craig et al. Washington May 10, 1938
Source: US Library of Congress (public domain)

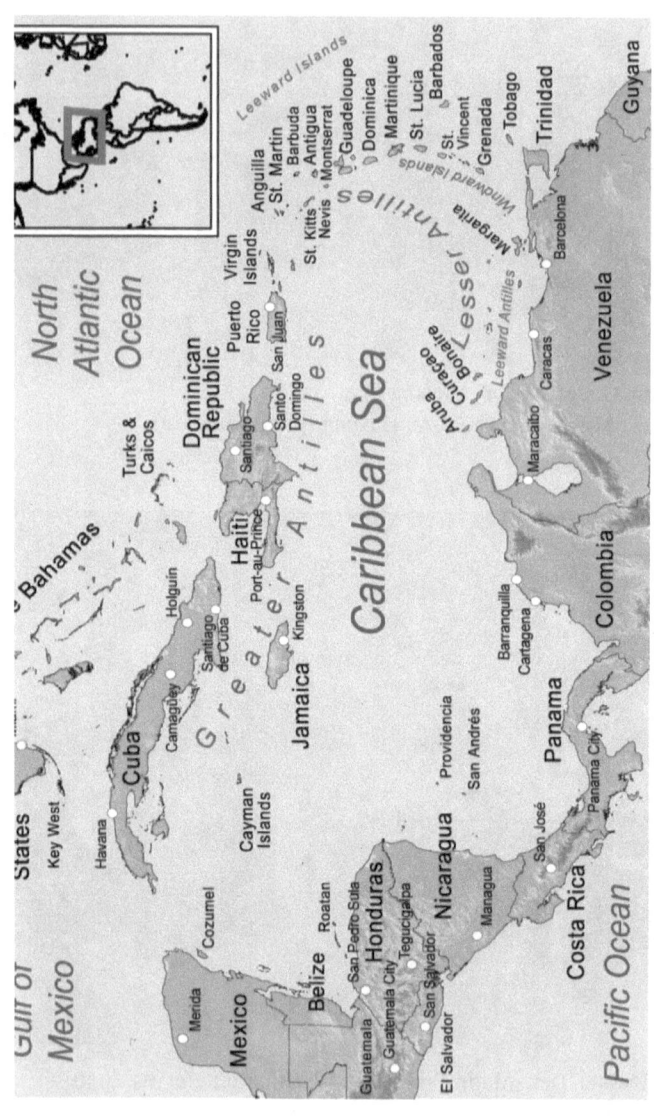

Caribbean Islands
Source: Courtesy of K. Musser (public domain)

1 Introduction

Cuba officially blames America's trade embargo for the difficulties it has in advancing its economy and the wellbeing of its people. Cuba has publically repeated its official position several times, and it has done this using the world's most recognised forum, the United Nations.

In a 2006 report to the UN, Cuba's First Deputy Foreign Minister Bruno Rodríguez-Parrilla proclaimed that,

> "The economic, trade and financial embargo, imposed by the government of the United States against Cuba, continues being the prime obstacle to the economic and social growth of the country." [1]

The UN has received similar reports every year since 1992, and each one has gained the General Assembly's overwhelming approval. [2]

It may seem obvious that America's embargo against Cuba has had far reaching and serious impact on the island's economy, but nobody has explained exactly why it is obvious.

No one has yet quantified the aggregate effect of the embargo on Cuba's economy.

The US government intended its embargo to act upon the Cuban populace by instilling general discontent and destabilizing political sentiments. Starting with the cancellation of American contracts to purchase Cuba's primary export commodity, sugar, the embargo soon extended to a prohibition on all bilateral trade and eventually to any Cuban related transaction involving American firms and other countries' firms operating in America (food, medicine, and humanitarian aid were excluded from these provisions to varying degrees over time). This act was supposed to result in one of two ultimate outcomes: a fundamental change in the regime's policies, or its complete overthrow. Although regime change never figured prominently in the early US record on the embargo, a continuing string of direct actions including the failed Bay of Pigs invasion provides evidence of the goal. The Cuban Democracy Act of 1992 finally codified the intended regime change into law, requiring free elections as one of several conditions for ending the embargo. [3]

Being a trade measure, the embargo's path to regime change should run straight through the economy, so the regime's survival with its policy structure intact can have one of two implications. Either the economy will have been little affected, or the Cuban people will have sided with their leaders and tacitly agreed to persevere in economic hardship.

Many observers adopt the latter position. That is, they take it to be obvious that the embargo has gravely damaged Cuba's economy, and that the government's vaunted policy of providing free education and health care sufficiently satisfies its people's sense of justice that their support of the leadership remains assured. This view may be encouraged by the abundant information describing the embargo's economic impact on specific sectors of the Cuban economy, and on specific instances of suffering. There is little dispute that such impacts exist, but they do not amount to a macro level or aggregate view.

Cuba's original revolutionary government has in fact maintained its ruling presence and communist structure under the US embargo for fifty years. Its policy behaviour has not changed, so it may seem reasonable to conclude that the Cuban people remain satisfied. After all, they have not risen against their leaders. But focusing solely on whether or not the regime's behaviour has changed misses the crucial step of assessing the real extent of economic impact. Did the people grant their loyalty to the regime even in the face of extraordinary economic suffering? Or did the presumed economic devastation never materialise?

The Cuban government's unwavering policy resolve over five decades could also suggest that the economy has not been critically upset. In other words, it is just as reasonable to conclude that the embargo has not had the significant macroeconomic effect intended by US sanctions. Observers may assume that the embargo has negatively affected Cuba's macro economy because the sanctions' scale and persistence make it seem reasonable to believe. Nevertheless, the fact remains that any such impact has never been directly or independently quantified.

An initial hint of the extent to which the embargo would polarise observers may be taken from the two countries' diametrically opposed views on the first trade measure, the 1960 US sugar import ban. A government sanctioned website presents Cuba's damning view of President Eisenhower's action:

"That [Eisenhower] Administration carried out a vast number of threatening actions, including economic coercion and attacks against Cuba's principal economic targets. The suspension of the Cuban sugar quota in the American market stands out among these acts of aggression." [4]

A US State Department assessment demonstrates its reservation toward the early trade sanction under consideration in 1959 (December 14):

"Any economic sanctions which are feasible would not have a very serious impact, but would be an irritant and probably counterproductive. A partial reduction of the Cuban sugar quota would be annoying to the Castro government but would have only a slight injurious effect on the Cuban economy. Even the total exclusion of Cuban sugar from the U.S. market—not considered feasible—would reduce Cuban national income by only about 5 per cent." [5]

Resolving these divergent views requires an independent economic appraisal.

* * *

America's 50 year trade embargo against Cuba, officially part of the US Foreign Assistance Act, is widely known to Cubans as el Bloqueo (the blockade). The terminology is not insignificant. The US refers to its sanctions against Cuba as an embargo. This means that trade restrictions or outright bans are imposed on either imports or exports according to the evolving legislation. Cuba refers to the sanctions in much broader terms, as a blockade, meaning that the US not only restricts its own trade with Cuba, but that it also interferes with the transactions of third party nations.

Cuba takes these sanctions as being an illegal act of undeclared warfare directly targeting the Cuban people, intended to deprive them of their free choice in domestic political affairs by making life difficult. Here the people's free choice refers to their right to support the revolutionary government unimpeded by foreign coercion.

From the American perspective, the embargo remains a justifiable action primarily on the grounds that the Cuban government confiscated US commercial possessions without compensation, allied itself with a foreign power hostile to the US and installed nuclear missiles capable of striking the US mainland. Furthermore, Cuba has supported other governments around the world in cases where the opportunity for revolution exists or where anti-American factions operate. The restraint of trade is intended by the US to pressure the Cuban people to urge an end to their one party government and restore confiscated property.

*   *   *

Trade is said to be the lifeblood of small economies and in this respect, it seems straightforward for economists and critics to view the embargo as the key destructive force in Cuba. With limited resources, small countries are forced to import several classes of goods. With limited scale, these small economies must specialise in a narrow range of activities for export. Restraint of trade should produce severe consequences.

Cuba, however, is not alone in claiming losses due to the embargo. Along with Cuba's claim of large scale losses, US firms point to their own forgone annual export revenue in the range of one billion dollars as a result of the embargo.

Even though the embargo was aimed in part at exacting compensation for confiscated US property in Cuba, one unintended consequence was that some US industrial sectors and several individual firms sustained ongoing losses in a bid to recoup past losses. American detractors of the embargo point to this doubling of losses as a negative consequence of a futile policy. Nevertheless, there need not be a net loss in global trade. Foreign firms could simply take over America's prohibited exports to Cuba and at least partially mitigate the macroeconomic impact on the island.

The ongoing US loss of Cuba's trade does not suggest that any balancing effect exists in the conflict between the two countries. In other words, it is not the case that US losses justify or offset Cuban losses. Rather it indicates the possibility that Cuba's trade merely shifts to other countries and mitigates US sanctions. Only an independent macro level analysis can verify the net effect.

*   *   *

Scores of books and journals present a social, cultural, or political analysis of the embargo, clearly showing that Cuba is of great interest. So, one would expect a body of economic literature to have developed over the decades, both from the embargo's supporters and detractors. At the national level, studies of trade flows and their contribution to GDP could easily be compiled by international agencies or universities. Well regarded trade models such as the Gravity Theory could be used to compare Cuba's external sector with its neighbours in order to verify Cuba's claims. Or more crucially, the government could use its own records and archives to analyse the country's macroeconomic performance before and after the embargo. The embargo carries the blame for wrecking the island's economy as well as forfeiting opportunities for a wide range of US business sectors, and yet a macroeconomic analysis of its impact remains virtually nonexistent.

While verbal commentary on Cuba's economic devastation abounds, it is never comprehensively quantified by government agencies, think tanks, academics, or journalists. Any existing analyses focus on partial time periods or specific industries. For example, the US embargo has been characterised as "the equivalent of economic warfare" and "a major destabilizing shock for the Cuban economy" by Tufts University professor Eliana Cardoso [6]. The period presented as evidence for this shock was 1966 - 1989, which excludes two central events in Cuba's modern history, namely the start of the embargo and the collapse of the Soviet Union. The briefness of the period is not a criticism of the author, though. The original data was in itself reconstructed from official fragments by trade economist Jorge F. Pérez-López, published in *Measuring Cuban Economic Performance*. The need for such reconstruction is typical of Cuban government data, which is widely distrusted due to historic inconsistency and secrecy. Cuba has variously used its own unique system of national accounts, revised its economic measures, suspended reporting, joined and left international agencies. University of Pittsburgh economist Carmelo Mesa-Lago provides some typical details in *The Economy of Socialist Cuba*. [7]

In any case, the data presented by Cardoso show that growth was negative for a mere three of the 24 years listed[8], and paradoxically, only one of those depressed years was in the 1960s, soon after the supposed shock was administered. Moreover, Cuba's growth performance through most of the 1970s would be the envy of most advanced economies.

The following growth series was derived from data in the aforementioned book (note that GSP is a concept sometimes used in communist economies, roughly corresponding to GDP in market economies):

Growth of Cuba's Gross Social Product (GSP)

1966	0.0 %	1978	- 2.4%
1967	8.0 %	1979	4.1 %
1968	1.9 %	1980	4.0 %
1969	- 1.8 %	1981	15.3 %
1970	14.8 %	1982	4.0 %
1971	8.1 %	1983	3.9 %
1972	14.9 %	1984	6.2 %
1973	15.6 %	1985	3.5 %
1974	12.4 %	1986	2.0 %
1975	4.0 %	1987	- 4.8 %
1976	0.9 %	1988	1.4 %
1977	18.1 %	1989	0.0 %

Not only do these data show a mere three years of negative growth, but there is just one such year in any one decade. A convincing case for the embargo's macroeconomic devastation has yet to be made.

With an opposing conclusion, the US International Trade Commission published one relevant report in 2001. [9] It vaguely concludes that the embargo, "... generally had a minimal overall impact on the Cuban economy." [10] This is the only existing analysis of the embargo's economic effects but its narrow focus is limited to bilateral trade in specific sectors. Moreover, it only briefly mentions the pre-embargo economy so it cannot directly quantify the aggregate or long term effects of American sanctions against Cuba.

Underlying the lack of published analysis are the serious problems associated with Cuban economic statistics. The regime changed in 1959 and data collection was understandably postponed. Further interruptions were imposed by the government during the early 1960s. A new system of national accounts using the communist concept of gross social product (GSP) was later implemented, making official data incompatible with that of most other countries as well as pre-revolution economic data. The reporting of currency units shifts from constant to current pesos along with midstream currency revaluations such that the interpretation of official statistics can be unreliable. The result is that even the most basic measures, such as GDP before and after the embargo, must be reconstructed from alternative sources or be estimated. Many observers may simply presume that the embargo caused Cuba's poor performance, even though its economy has seldom been quantitatively compared with its non-embargoed peers to confirm that they fared better. Did they fare better? This potentially informative avenue remains unexplored.

The importance of a macroeconomic analysis stems from Cuba's unique political situation. Its government has declared itself the sole protector of its people's welfare by virtue of having overthrown the previous US allied dictatorship in the 1959 revolution. It has also assumed and retained exclusive control in all domestic and international economic matters. As a result, the government became the agent responsible for its people's economic outcome, both individually and collectively.

At the micro economic level of the household and the firm, and extending to industrial sectors, a great deal of historical and current data suggests that the embargo has done harm by denying trade in specific commodities, products, and services. But owing to the government's exclusive control, it alone holds the power to distribute economic benefits. It alone decides the macro issues of 'guns and butter', how many soldiers it sends abroad to support the global revolution versus how much its people will eat. So if Cuba's literacy rate, infant mortality rate and average lifespan are favourable, then the government can justifiably take credit, provided these features were not inherited from the previous regime. But if Cuba's food rations and citizens are too thin, then the government cannot avoid the responsibility that comes along with its total macroeconomic control.

Thus the key to understanding the embargo's true effect lies in the economy's aggregate size relative to the population. After all, if the embargo decimated the economic output of the 'average' person then the government had little to distribute to each real person. On the other hand, if the total losses arising from the embargo were counteracted by other economic forces, then observable deprivations could only be the result of the government's economic policies. Furthermore, a focus on the macroeconomic level clearly reveals whether shifts in the output trend correspond with embargo timing.

The Cuban government repeatedly claims that explicit economic harm stems from America's trade embargo. In 2006 First Deputy Foreign Minister Bruno Rodríguez-Parrilla itemised Cuba's sectoral losses totalling $86 billion over 45 years. [11] But he did not include offsetting gains from substitute trade, preferential trade with new allies or outright countermeasures from other sympathetic countries. Nor has he made any pre-embargo comparisons that might provide corroborating evidence of an economic shock. Cuba's government has also published a small number of unverifiable summaries such as an embargo related report to the UN in 2005, but has otherwise been silent on the overall economic impact. [12] Finally, Cuba's claims have never been independently quantified. After a history of partial information, a fragmented analysis, and a seeming gap in impartiality, the embargo's macroeconomic impact deserves a fresh look.

The American U2 spy plane.
Source: © The National Security Archive, The George Washington University (GWU).

Kennedy, Gromyko and Dobrynin at the White House, Oct. 18, 1962 (Kennedy does not reveal that he knows about the missiles).
Source: © The National Security Archive, GWU.

2 The Data Problem

A country's economic information is normally compiled by its own government but long run economic data on Cuba do not exist. The next best source for economic data is supra-national organizations. Within this category the World Bank provides the broadest coverage, but Cuba withdrew its membership on November 14, 1960.

The United Nations remains the only readily accessible data aggregator with which Cuba participates. Although UN data include detailed breakdowns of GDP by activity, they only reach back to 1970. This lacks the pre-revolutionary scope that economists need to discern the onset of the embargo's potential impacts.

Finally, some universities compile economic research databases such as the widely used Penn Table. This data, however, depends on inputs from some of the supra-national sources such as the UN and is therefore similarly limited in its time span. The farthest reaching in time is from the late economic historian Angus Maddison of Groningen University (Netherlands) who independently compiled estimates on Cuba extending back to 1929, and some Caribbean islands back to 1950. These, however, only cover GDP, meaning that specific economic sectors such as trade movements cannot be assessed.

So, if comprehensive long run data do not exist and the official pre-revolution data cannot be used, how can Cuba's economy be assessed before and after the embargo? There is no alternative than to combine partial data sets from the UN, Maddison and other agency sources to compare key aspects of its economy with other countries. Partial data is limited either in its timeframe or in the range of factors it addresses, but it can support multiple analyses that tell a cohesive story. Three geographic scales, national, regional, and global, can also be analysed using such data.

At the national level Cuba's pre-embargo economic growth from 1929 is compared with its own post-embargo growth using Maddison's data. At the regional level Cuba's growth from 1950 is compared with its immediate neighbours using Maddison's data, and confirmed using overlapping UN data. These neighbours, the islands of the Greater Antilles, are the largest

Caribbean economies: Jamaica, Dominican Republic, and Puerto Rico. At the global level, Cuba's industrial structure and trade from 1970 are compared with all world countries using UN data. These partial data sets can identify macroeconomic anomalies indicating the embargo's effects on Cuba.

Angus Maddison's time series of Cuban population and estimated GDP predates the embargo by 30 years and runs to 2008. This is the only continuous series covering multiple decades both pre and post embargo so it can reveal growth trends in GDP per capita that might be associated with the embargo or other world events. Maddison's data also include an averaged group of Latin American countries, useful both as a comparator and to avoid misdiagnosis. For instance, if Cuba's growth uniquely plummeted after the embargo started, then the embargo could be a contributing cause. But if neighbouring non-embargoed economies also declined, then such a case becomes less plausible.

Exports are especially important to the embargo question because the supposed mechanism behind economic harm to Cuba centres on the restraint of its trade with the US. The US Census Bureau compiles a panel of goods import and export volumes with each of its trading partners. This can indicate the effect of biased American purchasing preference and geographic proximity. If, for example, exporting goods to the US is shown to correlate strongly with other countries' economic performance, then the embargo may credibly be said to have detracted from Cuba's GDP by barring such exports. Conversely, if exports to the US are not correlated with economic performance, then the embargo against Cuba would seem less relevant.

Various institutional sources have compiled sugar trade data that can also provide a more detailed perspective on this formerly crucial industrial sector. Sugar was Cuba's key export commodity for decades, making it a useful indicator of the embargo's impact throughout the revolutionary transition period of the 1960s.

A country's industrial structure can be represented by the share of agriculture in its GDP. Because agriculture is the most ancient major industry, the degree of industrial development within a country can be gauged by how far its economy is biased away from agriculture. Cuba is the only country subject to continuous US sanctions for 50 years, so if the embargo is truly harmful, then its development would likely be impaired and its share of agriculture in GDP should stand out conspicuously from the global trend. But if Cuba's structure aligns with other countries, then the embargo would appear less impactful. To compare industrial structure, UN statistics which are available from 1970 are suitable as they cover most of the embargo period. [13]

The UN's Human development Index forms the final major element in assessing the embargo's impact. Although not a strictly economic indicator, the HDI includes gross national income per capita along with education and longevity. The HDI database permits a comparison of Cuba and most countries of the world over the recent decades for which it is available. Its application here is twofold. First, it can confirm or deny the other economic indicators and their sources, thus improving confidence in drawing a conclusion. Second, this globally recognised index extends the analysis beyond the economic realm to address human wellness outcomes at a national aggregate level.

In summary, the lack of comprehensive long term economic data leaves no alternative than to infer the embargo's effects from partial data sets of various indicators. None of these comparisons can be decisive on its own, though. For instance, if trade trends contradict GDP growth trends, then the embargo impact would remain ambiguous. The embargo's effects can only be confirmed or refuted if each element, GDP per capita, trade and structure, suggests the same conclusion.

* * *

One potentially controversial point about the dating of a key event should be considered before proceeding with the analysis. The official start date of the embargo can be interpreted as any one of a number of legislative or executive acts. Enabling legislation such as the Foreign Assistance Act of 1961 might be invoked as the starting point, or it might be an executive proclamation that executes a specific provision within the Act.

The embargo starting point may also be taken as May 24, 1962, the date on which the US formally suspended the most important trade designations granted to Cuba, namely preferential tariff treatment and Most Favored Nation status. Prior to that action, the US president was authorised to impose a total embargo on Cuba but had not done so.

The US Foreign Assistance Act of 1961 (Section 620) requires that,

> "No assistance shall be furnished under this Act to the present government of Cuba. As an additional means of implementing and carrying into effect the policy of the preceding sentence, the President is authorised to establish and maintain a total embargo upon all trade between the United States and Cuba." [14]

Nevertheless, the US enacted significant partial sanctions as far back as 1960 (see Appendix 1 below), as confirmed by a Cuban official at the UN:

> "Although the total blockade on trade between Cuba and the United States was formally decreed by an Executive Order issued by President John F. Kennedy on 3 February 1962, measures that are part of the blockade were put in place just a few weeks after the triumph of the Cuban Revolution on 1 January 1959." [15]

On July 6th 1960, the US cut its sugar imports from Cuba by over one half, and thereby took the first practical economic step against the new regime. Furthermore, the US banned its own exports to Cuba, and reduced the sugar quota to zero by presidential order on October 19, 1960. The embargo was effectively in place. Because sugar exports to the US were a key element in Cuba's trade, it is reasonable to assess the impact of US sanctions starting from the date of this sugar import ban. 1960 is used as the embargo start date in the following analysis.

3 Cuba's Unlikely Growth

Economic growth has not eluded Cuba. Instead the trouble lay in its inability to sustain its growth episodes, avoiding extended stagnation and brief, severe contraction. Two lost decades with near zero growth, the 1950s and 1960s, were followed by two growth decades and the catastrophic post-Soviet plunge of 37% in GDP per capita over the subsequent four years. That single decline dragged Cuba's output back almost fifty years to 1946 levels. There is no question as to whether Cuba's economy has been a disaster, but rather why. What caused Cuba's ruinous economic stagnation and contraction?

The easy and wrong answer is the embargo. For the entire decade immediately prior to the revolution and the embargo, per capita GDP changed very little as its annual growth averaged 0.54%. Nearly the same flat outcome followed in the post-revolution decade, -0.22% per year. In other words, economic growth was virtually zero both with and without the embargo for two consecutive decades. There was no sudden decline in growth upon the 1960 embargo onset, and no change throughout the next decade. The reasons for such poor results differed drastically from the 1950s to the 1960s, but merely prolonging a pre-existing stagnation is not what economists, journalists, and critics have in mind by suggesting that the embargo inflicted a catastrophic shock.

Table 1: Tracking Cuba's economic growth, before and during the embargo

GDP per capita and its growth (constant 1990 G-K $)					
Period	Average annual growth rate	Total growth over the period	GDP per capita start of period	GDP per capita end of period	Notes
1929 - 1959	0.78 %	26 %	$ 1,639	$ 2,067	Pre embargo
1959 - 1989	1.23 %	44 %	$ 2,067	$ 2,982	Embargo
1989 - 1994	- 8.89 %	- 37 %	$ 2,982	$ 1,872	Soviet collapse
1994 - 2008	5.12 %	101 %	$ 1,872	$ 3,208	Post Soviet

Source: derived from Maddison's GGDC database [16]

Table 1 shows that during the first three decades of embargo, Cuba's output per capita grew somewhat faster than during three decades prior to the embargo: 1.23 % vs. 0.78 % per year, on average. By this preliminary measure, the embargo does not seem to have impaired economic growth in the longer term.

Furthermore, Cuba was able to grow under many different conditions including the interwar years, the Soviet and post-Soviet periods, embargo or no embargo. And parceled in this way, its growth trend continued to accelerate in each period with one brief exception. The main interruption in Cuban growth was due to the shock of the Soviet Union's collapse.

Although the economy often faltered, this was to be the sole period of sustained double digit contraction since the Great Depression. The collapse of the USSR led to the collapse of Cuba's main export market along with its main source of imports. By 1989 trade accounted for nearly 70% of Cuba's GDP, and exports alone were 31% of GDP. The economic impact was devastating, with an average annual decline in GDP per capita of 8.89% over a six year span.

Meanwhile the embargo remained in place but with two significant changes to come. First the US tightened the embargo with the Torricelli Act in October 1992. Torricelli came after most of Cuba's output decline had occurred, so the act was clearly not implicated in this contractionary episode. A further embargo tightening came in March 1996 with the Helms-Burton Act. But instead of receding, Cuba's growth shot up to 7.4% in real terms that year, settled for two years and then resumed a rapidly rising trend. Even with the intensified embargo and the loss of Soviet trade, Cuba's growth returned at an unprecedented average rate of over 5% per year starting in 1996.

Cuba's average growth in real GDP per capita throughout the entire embargo era, 1960-2008 was a moderate 1.27 % per year. While not a stellar performance, this positive outcome certainly cannot be considered a disaster.

A simple thought experiment can help to discern the embargo's role more precisely. Consider a hypothetical case of eliminating only the Soviet collapse. Cuba would have grown at nearly double its historical rate, 2.14% per year. It would have had over 50% more annual output. In other words, a heavy reliance on the Soviet Union suddenly cost Cuba half a century of economic growth. The catastrophic decline of 1991-93 was entirely due to events in the Soviet sphere whereas the embargo's onset and reinforcements did not even register.

Combined with Cardoso's growth tally of 1966 to 1989 above, Maddison's 48 year data in table 1 provides the first evidence based indication of the embargo's minimal real impact.

*   *   *

A First Note on Exports

Does Cuba's export trend confirm Maddison's generally positive growth trend from table 1 above? Export trends are particularly relevant because the US embargo severed Cuban trade with its largest partner. About 50% of Cuba's exports formerly went to the US, and sugar was 80-90% of the total. The clear expectation is that exports would drop and growth would suffer. Instead, the US cancelled its sugar contracts in July 1960 but Cuba's export tonnage remained in its normal historic range because the Soviet Union immediately increased purchases to over 51% of Cuba's sugar exports. Preferentially priced US sales were quickly replaced by socialist country sales, so sugar exports were unaffected for the next quarter century. [17]

Total exports of goods and services per capita maintained a declining trend from their 1948 peak until bottoming in 1962 (see figure 1).[18] That decline started even before the Batista regime of the 1950s, far too early to have been caused by the 1960 embargo.

Figure 1: Comparing long term regional trends in exports per capita

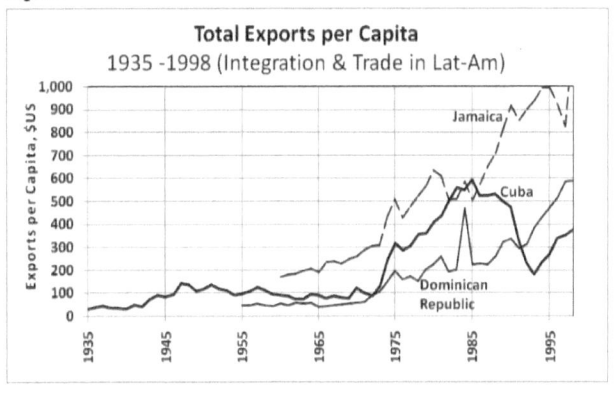

Source: derived from *Integration and Trade in Latin America* [19]

Strangely, the resumption of Cuba's rise in exports coincided with the official start of the embargo in 1962, further undermining claims of its great harm.

Moreover, the embargo cannot have caused Cuba's GDP stagnation during the 1960s while suddenly becoming immaterial in its higher growth 1970s, 1980s, late 1990s and beyond. Why not? Because the key mechanisms by which Cuba was supposed to have been impaired, restricted export markets and greater costlier trade distance, were constant throughout the embargo whereas exports per capita were increasing. If the embargo was strongly effective, exports and growth should at least have remained stagnant.

Could it be instead that Cuban GDP had indeed stagnated due to the new trade embargo and then readjusted by the 1970s? To the contrary, Cuba's long declining exports of the pre-embargo years rebounded in 1963. So if there was any adjustment, it was more as though the embargo pushed Cuban exports upward. Even the trend in exports as a share of GDP was stable or rising from the start of the embargo until the late 1980s. The Soviet Union's collapse caused the only major drop in Cuba's export share of GDP.

The rise of Cuban exports into the 1970s and early 1980s was closely replicated by

Jamaican and Dominican Republic exports. This suggests that the three countries might have been involved in a sub-regional pattern instead of an isolated national one. The implication may be that the embargo impact on exports was merely masked, and that its true economic harm manifested in another way. This possibility along with Cuba's uniquely plunging exports in the late 1980s is addressed in further detail below.

How plausible is the preliminary idea that the embargo did not affect Cuba's exports and growth? In a study of import-export sanctions, Stockholm University economist Per Lundborg describes the 1948 Soviet embargo against Yugoslavia as having no net effect. Although Yugoslavia claimed a $400 million loss due to the embargo, this was offset by increased aid and loans from Western countries in response. In sum, Yugoslavia registered a net gain of 2.5% of GDP. [20]

Lundborg finds that negative impacts are evident within some sectors of an embargoed economy, especially in cases where the sanctions are imposed by a large economy on a small dependent trade partner. The mechanism is economically straightforward. The smaller partner faces fewer buyers for its tradable goods and its selling prices are bid down. It also faces fewer suppliers for its import needs and must offer higher prices. Meanwhile, if shipping distances increase, transport costs also rise. As inevitable as this process may seem, though, the decisions of other countries can easily subvert it. For instance, the target country may receive more favourable terms from its allies due to political considerations, or it may attract new opportunistic trading partners that offset the embargo losses. The overall policy usually fails if a significant number of nations do not act in concert, and the net macroeconomic effect on Cuba may be nil for the same reasons.

The Official Record on Growth

Cuba's statistical agency, Oficina Nacional de Estadisticas (ONE), publishes a series of selected macroeconomic indicators annually. These often consist of strictly limited time spans, five or six years, precluding a long term analysis. Nevertheless, a comparison of two overlapping time series may be instructive regarding the contents and the consistency of data.

The following samples (table 2 and 3) each consist of a six year series. Taking gross product per capita as the indicator, the decade following two important embargo reinforcements (1992, 1996) showed the following values and growth rates.

Table 2: Cuba's output from the official 2009 Yearbook (at constant 1997 peso prices)

Year	Output	Growth %
2004	2,922	
2005	3,247	11.1
2006	3,639	12.1
2007	3,904	7.3
2008	4,066	4.1
2009	4,124	1.4

Source: Oficina Nacional de Estadisticas
www.one.cu/aec2009/esp/20080618_tabla_cuadro.htm

Table 2 shows that Cuba's indicated growth rates are higher than those achieved by most countries of the world and are about in line with high growth countries such as China and Brazil. These figures also showed a reduced but still positive growth rate in the global recession's first two years, 2008-9, during which most advanced economies registered severe contractions.

In the 2009 Yearbook shown in table 2, the output level figures were significantly revised upward from the 2006 Yearbook shown in table 3 below:

Table 3: Cuba's output from the official 2006 Yearbook (at constant 1997 peso prices)

Year	Output	Growth %
2001	2,818	
2002	2,862	1.6
2003	2,963	3.5
2004	3,117	5.2
2005	3,484	11.8
2006	3,920	12.5

Source: Oficina Nacional de Estadisticas
www.one.cu/aec2006/anuariopdf2006/capitulo4/IV-3.pdf

The growth rates from the two yearbooks above can be compared in the overlapping years, 2005 and 2006. Although the output levels were revised upward in the later publication, the indicated growth rates remained at approximately the same high level that rank among the best in the world.

How does the official growth data compare to Maddison and UN data?

	Maddison	UN	ONE
2002	1.1	1.2	1.6
2003	2.5	3.6	3.5
2004	4.8	5.6	5.2
2005	11.6	11.1	11.8
2006	11.7	12.0	12.5
2007	7.0	7.2	7.3
2008	3.8	4.3	4.1

Angus Maddison, highly regarded as a strict numerical analyst, often produced independent estimates of a country's industrial output where significant doubts surrounded the official figures. Even so, in the list above, Maddison shows only marginally lower growth than Cuban government data in each year, with no greater than a 1% difference. The UN's data is virtually identical to Cuba's official data, so there is no significant dispute between the three sources on the annual growth rate throughout this period. Again, that growth rate is positive and nontrivial in each year. In addition, the growth trend is generally rising and even returned a substantial positive value through the global recession's first year. So if Cuba's economic growth rate does not seem impaired in its own right, then the remaining issue is that of finding evidence for the embargo's purportedly devastating impact on its output levels and growth relative to other countries.

To say that the embargo was a serious impediment to Cuba's economy is to maintain a myopic focus on Cuba's poor output level instead of its growth record. Table 1 showed per capita output to rise and fall substantially through the late 20th century, so the picture is mixed within Cuba's own history. It is also mixed in relation to its regional counterparts. Cuba currently ranks better than midway among Latin American countries in GDP per capita (ninth of 19), but sits third from the bottom in a sampling of 20 major Caribbean islands. [21] It may be this low relative position that inclines observers to believe that Cuba is poor and that the embargo is to blame.

At first glance, Cuba's aggregate output per capita does not show any evidence of being depressed compared to its non-embargoed Latin American neighbours including one of its closest comparators, Dominican Republic. At $3,800 Cuba's 2005 output slightly exceeded Latin America's average of $3,710 (UN data in $US).

But a comparison with the Caribbean island countries gives a very different result. Cuba ranks 3rd from the bottom among the UN's list of 20 islands in the region whose average GDP per capita more than triples Cuba's at $13,000. These are primarily small rapidly changing economies focused almost exclusively on the services sector and especially on banking, insurance, and luxury tourism. The exceptions, Dominican Republic and Jamaica, are Cuba's true peers in economic scale with very similar population and GDP levels. And Cuba performed at a level just between these peers in 2005.

While it may seem plausible that the embargo held Cuba back from the economic progress of the small islands, one political concept should entirely dispel the idea. It remains virtually impossible to imagine that without the embargo, Cuba would have made a similar shift toward the small islands' financial industries that utterly contradict a central tenet of the Cuban revolution: developing the socialist 'New Man'. This ideal citizen was to have laboured at real industrial production motivated by his nation's welfare and that of his fellow man instead of his own material gain. The economic policy most opposed to Cuba's steadfast industrial goals was that of its small island neighbours that engaged in shuffling financial accounts or developing vacation real estate for foreign tourists. Cuba's wealthiest neighbours now generate over ten times its economic output but, absent the embargo, it is clear that Cuba would not have taken their route.

As to the growth record, the forgoing figures clearly do not support the view of Cuba as a country beset by economic warfare. Stagnation has long since receded, becoming a feature of the revolutionary transition era, while the severe contraction of the early 1990s now appears to have been an isolated event. All of the data sources agree on Cuba's sustained economic growth.

The data, however, may suggest the possibility that the government has exaggerated its economic position or the possibility that Cuba and its allies have counteracted any trade constraints imposed by the US. But, since the impartial and sceptical sources (UN and Maddison) agree with official Cuban government data, exaggeration seems unlikely. The remaining conclusion is that according the government's own statistics, the US embargo has not constrained Cuba's growth rate in the Torricelli/Helms era of heightened trade restrictions.

In reviewing Cuba's growth record over recent decades, the first indication is that the embargo does not seem to have affected the economy in aggregate. The timing of embargo related events such as the first 1960 sanction and subsequent reinforcements do not support the common perception of its great harm. Furthermore, a plausible mechanism exists to explain this outcome; the target country, Cuba, has found alternative trading partners to substitute for the loss of US markets. Even so, this does not constitute sufficient evidence of the embargo's ineffectiveness. Even if the embargo did not have a direct depressing impact, then perhaps it blocked Cuba from the growth enjoyed by similar countries in the region. The following section more fully explores Cuba's growth record in this wider regional context.

4 Comparing Regional Growth

Prior to the 1959 revolution, Cuba's level of output per capita ranked about midway between the small Latin-American and small Caribbean countries.[22] Maddison shows that Cuba turned out neither a stellar nor dismal economic performance within the region. But its post revolution output remained stagnant for a decade and then permanently lagged both peer groups.

In 1961 Cuba's output level slipped below Latin America's average and was trapped there for the next 46 years. While Cuba's output grew by 50%, the average Caribbean economy grew over 100%. By 2006, the average Caribbean country had about triple Cuba's per capita output level. The impression is of a middling performer that not only failed to keep up, but also lost its capability to recover.

Table 4: Comparing Cuba's growth with the economies of its region

Period	Cuba	Average of 21 Small Caribbean Countries	Average of 15 Small Latin American Countries	Average of 8 Large Latin American Countries	Notes on Cuba
1940-1959	2.9%	n/a	n/a	2.28 %	Pre-embargo
1970-1991	1.4%	1.26 %	1.06 %	1.24 %	Embargo with Soviet aid
1994 - 2008	5.1%	2.09 %	1.75 %	1.72 %	Embargo & no Soviet aid

Average Annual Growth of GDP per Capita (constant 1990 G-K $)

Source: derived from Maddison's GGDC database

But certain periods of growth in GDP per capita tell a different tale. For example, table 4 shows that from 1940 until 1959 Cuba's 2.9% annual growth rate nearly doubled the world rate of 1.66%. It also exceeded the large Latin American country group. Likewise, Cuba's growth exceeded the averages of both Caribbean and Latin American groups during the 1970s and 1980s and even more so after the Soviet Union collapsed (5.1% annually over fourteen years). Far from being economically hindered, Cuba's growth potential seemed ever-present. This reinforces a seeming contradiction between Cuba's low level of economic output and its recurring capacity for growth.

The key question remains whether or not the embargo affected the Cuban macro-economy. If it did, the mechanism must be identified. The official Cuban claim is that its economy was impaired by forced exclusion from US trade. This increases Cuba's cost of goods through normal economic channels: increased transport cost and reduced supply opportunities. This claim can be tested by comparing Cuba's economic performance with neighbours that enjoy greater US trade integration.

The Greater Antilles islands are useful comparators due to their similar location, climate, colonial history, and industrial base. Three of the islands share Spanish as a national language. Puerto Rico is a US possession so, in absolute contrast with a trade isolated Cuba, completely integrated with the US both politically and economically. It should hold a great economic advantage. Jamaica may benefit in trade by sharing English as its main language with the nearby US. Dominican Republic resembles Cuba in its location, geographic scale and population so these physical features are likely insignificant in economic terms. The embargo is expected to eclipse all of these factors because it acts directly upon a key Cuban economic activity, trade.

By Maddison's data, Cuba, Dominican Republic, and Jamaica turned out approximately the same range of GDP per capita from 1960 to 2008 (see figure 2, below).

Figure 2: the longest series of comparable GDP data

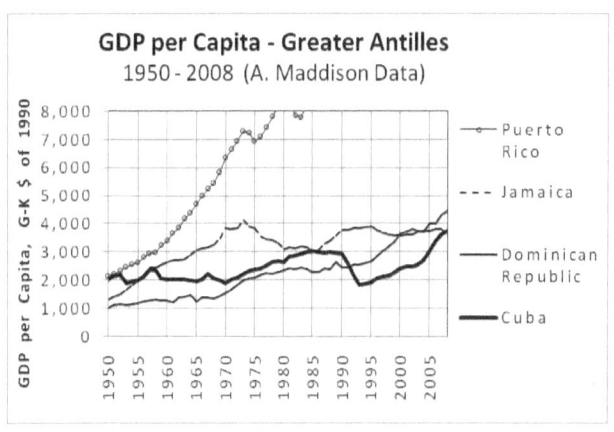

Source: derived from Maddison's GGDC database

Cuba started the period ranked second and ended the period ranked second. Each country has occupied first, second and third place at various times. They started out together in the low GDP category and ended up there together. Cuba and Jamaica produced $3,764 and $3,668 per capita in 2008 while Dominican Republic was only slightly higher at $4,464. Puerto Rico also started at the same low output level, but it seems that its key distinction was not the rate of growth but consistency of growth. Why? Because at various times each of the others also grew at the same or higher rate than Puerto Rico but did not maintain it. Puerto Rico's advantage in US integration is not in question though. The question is whether the embargo against Cuba produced a crushing macroeconomic shock and lower output than its independent non-embargoed neighbours. Compared to Jamaica and Dominican Republic, the GDP data do not show the 1960 embargo having any discernable impact on Cuba. Cuba's overall growth lay between its two neighbours.

Verifying Maddison's data using UN data reveals a similar story but shows Cuba even more favourably. See figure 3 below, which starts from 1970.

Figure 3: verifying Maddison's GDP data, 1970-2008

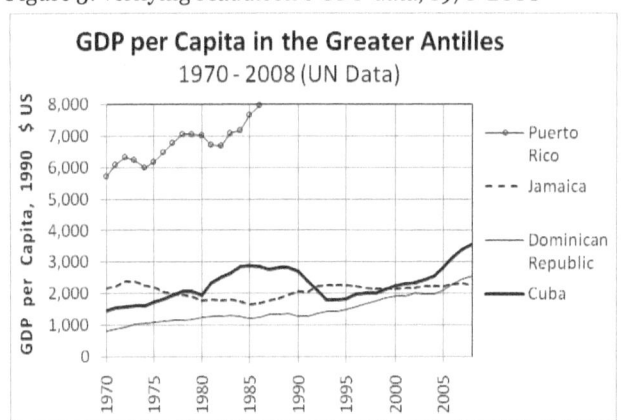

Source: derived from UN National Accounts Database

While Puerto Rico is alone at a much higher level, the other three islands are tightly grouped. Cuba starts the period in the middle rank between Dominican Republic and Jamaica, but ends the period ranking first. Dominican Republic makes progress, but lags Cuba throughout. Only Jamaica fails to progress at all over the period, dropping to the bottom rank.

Table 5: comparing Cuba's growth with its neighbours, the Greater Antilles

Average Ann. GDP per Capita Growth (1990 G-K $)					
Period	Cuba	Jamaica	Domin. Republic	Puerto Rico	Notes on Cuba
1950 - 1959	0.11%	7.49 %	2.51 %	4.69 %	Pre-revolution decade
1959 - 1969	- 0.2%	3.19 %	1.25 %	6.07 %	Decade of revolution &embargo
1969 - 1991	1.12%	0.38 %	2.39 %	2.79 %	Embargo; Soviet aid
1991 - 1994	- 10.2%	0.96 %	2.42 %	3.63 %	Soviet collapse
1994 - 2008	5.12 %	- 0.42 %	3.86 %	1.69 %	Embargo; no Soviet aid

Source: derived from Maddison's GGDC database

What about the growth pattern? It seems reasonable to expect that Cuba's worst circumstances for growth would be under the embargo, with no majority trading partner. And yet in the most recent period (1994-2008), with exactly those conditions and a tightened embargo, table 5 shows Cuba as having seen its highest growth ever. This argues against the idea of economic harm from restraint of trade.

Jamaica is free to trade with everyone in the world, has an English language advantage in US markets and is even a member of the Commonwealth since 1962, and yet has seen a steadily deteriorating growth rate for over half a century. Table 5 shows Jamaica with a virtually stalled economy over the 40 years since 1969. Dominican Republic and Puerto Rico are more typical in that they had fluctuating positive growth over the decades although Puerto Rico clearly has an economic advantage in being a fully integrated US possession.

Cuba, Dominican Republic, and Jamaica were tightly grouped in output terms but how did Cuba's compare with its neighbours and even the US in growth? Did Cuban growth consistently rank last due to the embargo? From 1970 to 2008 UN statistics show Cuba outpacing each country (individually) in the majority of years. Cuban growth outpaced Puerto Rico in 22 years. It outpaced the US in 20 years. It outpaced Dominican Republic in 21 years, and Jamaica in 30 out of those 37 years. Cuba even ranked first out of all five countries in 14 of those years. Finally, Cuba's total compound growth for the period was higher than Jamaica, Puerto Rico, and the US (146% vs. 4%, 127% and 109% respectively).

Cuba has clearly shown the ability to match or exceed other countries in growth. It does not portray a hobbled economy unable to produce. Instead, Cuba's ongoing macroeconomic progress was interrupted by a prolonged stagnation and a rare but extraordinarily severe downturn. Its inconsistent performance resolves the apparent contradiction of Cuban growth capability and poor output.

Aside from Cuba, Haiti was the only Caribbean country to decline from 1990 to 1993. Thus its decline was not part of a wider regional trend. This reveals that while the embargo was constant, something else changed for Cuba. That detrimental change was the Soviet collapse.

Did other Soviet related economies also contract? If so, it would confirm the cause of Cuba's decline. Soviet influenced states such as Poland, Albania, Romania, Bulgaria, and Hungary, did indeed decline sharply in the early 1990s along with Cuba. In the rest of the world only Liberia, Mongolia, Haiti, Peru, Sudan, and Angola declined at such a steep rate, so Cuba's contraction was not part of a global one. There was also a recession in western countries but this was much shorter and milder, with no similar declines. Economic conditions around the world point to a reliance on the collapsing USSR as the cause of Cuba's decline.

Did the 1992 and 1996 embargo changes have any impact? The 1992 change was too late to have caused Cuba's decline that started in 1990. Furthermore, there was no drop in growth upon the 1996 tightening. So Cuba's decline seems to be solely as part of a Soviet related group. Its shock was primarily felt throughout Eastern Europe and only Cuba in the Caribbean. In contrast, the embargo has been a constant presence through which Cuba has grown, both before and after the Soviet crash.

Even the supposedly crucial Soviet trade subsidies of the 1970s and 1980s prove to be less than relevant in light of Cuba's high growth 1994-2008 post-Soviet period. Increased tourism, exports, and more open investment policies helped fuel Cuba's 5.1% annual average growth that greatly outstripped America and Puerto Rico, even in the face of the relentless embargo coupled with the Soviet loss. This outcome does not, however, decisively indicate a superior Cuban economic capability. Following the Soviet collapse, Cuba developed an ideologically based relationship with Venezuela's upcoming presidential candidate, Hugo Chávez. After winning the presidency in 1998 Chávez replaced the Soviet oil trade with Venezuelan supplies. Overall aid and trade assistance materialised and helped to partly fill the post Soviet gap. Again, it is not the case that the embargo has no effect, but rather that the macro effect is at least partly undone by opportunistic rivals.

Finally, it is worth noting that the embargo did not drive Cuba to align itself with the USSR, as Cuba took that action before the embargo. In February of 1960, Cuba and the USSR agreed to establish trade in sugar and crude oil. This was enacted while the US still officially recognised the new revolutionary government as the legitimate representative of the Cuban people. Cuba then restored diplomatic relations with the USSR in May of 1960 and confiscated US oil refineries in June, both prior to any US trade actions. The US reduced Cuba's sugar import quota later, in July. This means that the USSR was not initially approached by Cuba as a replacement for lost US trade, but it nevertheless became a heavy trade subsidiser and thus offset the embargo's impact from the early 1960s through the late 1980s.

José De Gregorio, former Vice-President of Chile's central bank, offers a summary statement on a key regional economic trend:

> "Latin America has been dominated by growth expansions that, more often than not, have ended in crises and protracted periods of stagnation". [23]

These two macroeconomic adversities, crisis and stagnation, hit Cuba in two important stages; during the revolutionary transition and the Soviet collapse. Many high income countries experience similar events but they very rarely run as deep or as long as the typical Latin American case. So this regional affliction seems to perfectly explain Cuba's low output level.

No Latin American countries were embargoed and yet they shared Cuba's economic malaise, or worse, for decades because they too suffered crisis and stagnation. This further undermines the idea of embargo induced macroeconomic impact on Cuba.

Even so, the embargo has not yet been eliminated as having affected the economy in aggregate because the US may employ less visible adverse economic practices against Latin America as a whole. The embargo's impact on Cuba may be clouded by the possibility of such practices so a global level analysis is needed.

Nikita Khrushchev in Berlin, 1963
Source: Deutsches Bundesarkiv (public domain)

Hugo Chávez in Porto Alegre, 2003
Source: Agência Brasil (public domain)

5 The Global Trade Surprise

Exporting to the US

In a 2004 report to the UN, the Cuban government briefly categorises the losses caused by the embargo. [24] The cumulative loss until 2003 is stated as $79.3 billion. Nearly half of the loss is shown as forgone export earnings of $36.2 billion. Although there are no specific grounds to doubt this figure, the report appears to ignore the fact that Cuba's exports have merely shifted to alternative countries.

Even though substitute markets were found, increased costs are likely to reduce Cuba's net export earnings. For example, in accordance with the well established Gravity Theory of trade, greater distances and shipping costs make Cuba a less desirable supplier to European markets than it was to American markets, so its exports may decline. Embargo provisions also penalise Cuba's trading partners that trade with America in an attempt to deter substitute markets from forming. Nevertheless, hidden benefits may offset these losses. Some countries such as Venezuela may be ideologically inclined to increase trade with Cuba precisely to thwart the embargo. Others may be attracted to Cuban goods due to the reduced price competition from America. The net effect of the embargo is clouded by these counter currents but may be revealed by Cuba's export trends.

Figure 4: the effect of exporting to the US on GDP per capita

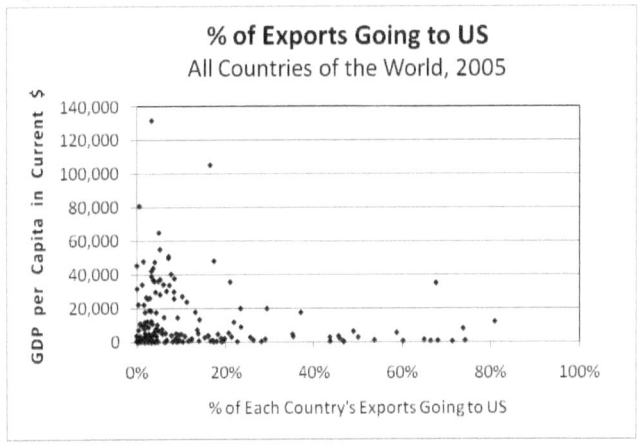

Sources:
1. Goods Exports derived from US Census Bureau
2. GDP per Capita derived from UN National Accounts Database [25]

Would exporting goods to the US be more advantageous to Cuba than its substitute exports to the rest of the world? Figure 4 shows the vast majority (31/36) of countries with high GDP per capita (over $20,000) have low exports to the US (under 10%). All of Western Europe, the world's wealthiest region, is at less than 8%. The majority (15/22) of countries with high (over 35%) exports to the US have lower economic output than Cuba. These include countries in Caribbean, South America, Central America, Africa and Asia. The suggestion is that high output per capita is not driven by exporting to America.

Globally, the correlation of all countries' US exports to GDP per capita is nearly random, but slightly negative at -0.106. This is indicated by the unpopulated upper-right region of the graph in figure 4. In short, exports to the US are not associated with prosperity at all, as the relation is virtually random.

Within the Caribbean, the negative correlation is very slightly stronger at -0.237. So increasing exports to the US is associated with decreasing GDP for this group, the opposite of the embargo's supposed economic harm mechanism. The data are weakly biased toward the likelihood that Cuba would have done worse by intensive trading with the US. Why would this be the case?

It is possible that more intense price competition within the US market reduces the value of a country's exports. After all, small nations do not wield as great a level of market power as the US.

Of course this weak correlation does not prove that increased exports to the US cause GDP per capita to decline in the exporting country. But it is also true that the correlation argues against the suggestion that the US market could be crucial to Cuba's economy.

Gravity and Exports to the US

Exports to the US are thought to be crucial to Cuba's growth, in large part because America is seen as Cuba's 'natural market' due to its size and physical proximity. The US dominates the world in size and can easily absorb exports from small economies. furthermore, Cuba lies a mere 130 miles off the Florida coast, so it should expect transport costs to be lower than those associated with any other major trading partner. Mexico lies at about the same distance but its output pales in comparison with the US.

The most important economic theory that addresses these trade parameters (size and distance) is the Gravity Theory. This theory holds that the influence exerted by trading economies on each other resembles the force of gravity in physics. That is, the force of gravity is a function of an object's mass and its distance to another object. In trade theory, the relation involves the volume of trade flow, size of GDP and distance between two countries. In its earliest form, 'distance' simply referred to the geographic distance between the countries as a way to capture all effects related to transportation costs and other trade inhibitors.

One indication of the theory's early crudeness involved the way it addressed large countries or bordering countries. For instance, Puerto Rico lies close to Miami and much of its economic connection stems from this minimal separation. But the theory assigned the distance between the countries as the distance between their capital cities, so Puerto Rico's distance from America was deemed to be from the island to Washington DC. This contributed to inaccuracy in prediction as well as some hesitation in adopting it. The case of a shared border such as Canada and the US created the absurd intuition that the distance between the countries was zero, while using the capital cities did little to address the reality of major regional markets.

Later refinements to the distance concept included all conceivable barriers to bilateral trade, collectively termed 'economic distance' or remoteness. Recent developments in gravity theory, though, have shown that the effects of multilateral trade barriers can be so significant as to overwhelm the importance of geographic distance.

Some early versions of the Gravity Theory of trade have had difficulty with accurate predictions because they naively used the distance between country capitals as the main determining factor. Of course, the distance between Havana and Washington D.C. is irrelevant to trade as long as the bulk of goods and tourism would transit through Florida. The key US port of Miami should be used instead. With this basic parameter in place, the percentage of each country's exports to the US can be assessed more directly and may indicate whether the embargo suppressed Cuba's industrial capacity and output.

Table 6 (below) shows the two previously mentioned embargo related factors that can help assess the potential impact on Cuba: exports to the US and distance from each country to the key

US port of Miami. These may indicate the effect of transport costs imposed by the embargo by forcing trade to shift to further destinations.

A key data set comes from the annual UN report, *Latin America and the Caribbean in the World Economy*. The 2005-6 report [26] lists each Latin American country's exports to the US as a percentage of its total exports. Although Jamaica and Puerto Rico are not in the Latin American group of countries, they are included in the table to continue the previous regional comparison.

Table 6: the effect of exporting to the US on Latin American GDP per capita

	% Exports to US	GDP per capita	Distance (miles)
Cuba	-	3,787	-
Paraguay	3	1,266	6,419
Argentina	11	4,728	5,667
Bolivia	14	1,040	3,853
Panama	15	4,786	1,214
Chile	16	7,257	3,853
Brazil	19	4,721	4,576
Uruguay	22	5,221	5,562
Peru	30	2,911	2,555
Colombia	42	3,217	1,096
Costa Rica	45	4,614	1,093
Ecuador	47	2,847	1,690
Guatemala	50	2,141	1,151
Venezuela	59	5,445	1,254
El Salvador	61	2,560	2,037
Nicaragua	63	955	1,888
Honduras	75	1,428	765
Dom. Rep.	78	3,542	799
Mexico	86	8,096	809
(Jamaica	10	4,180	730)

Sources:
1. Goods Exports derived from US Census Bureau;
2. 2005 GDP per Capita derived from UN National Accounts Database, in $ current. [27]

Cuba ranks in the middle of the group with respect to its GDP per capita, while its exports to the US are of course, ranked last with an absolute total of zero. Meanwhile, Cuba's immediate neighbour, Dominican Republic, sells 78% of its exports the US although it doesn't get a corresponding boost in output; its GDP per capita is about equal to Cuba's.

For a contrasting example, Honduras sells 75% of its exports to the US while its GDP per capita is less than half of Cuba's. In both cases, as well as seven other countries in the group, high exports to the US do not have the benefit that is intuitively expected. Moreover, five countries with less than 20% of their exports going to the US have higher output than Cuba. It is clear that exporting to the US is no economic panacea.

To summarise the forgoing export data, the correlation of exports to the US with country GDP per capita is very nearly nonexistent, -0.016. But correlation can in some cases be an overly generalised measure, and it may not capture the effect of US destined Caribbean exports. The distance between the US and each country could also play a direct role.

The correlation between shipping distance and the percentage of a country's exports to the

US is strong and inverse at -0.782. So, as expected, greater distance is associated with less export flow and there are no glaring exceptions. Having confirmed this obvious relationship, it may also seem obvious that greater distance could be associated with less economic output due to less export volume. The data, however, do not show any sign of such a trend. This correlation is also practically nonexistent (-0.012) meaning that physical proximity to the US market does not assure increased prosperity to an exporting country.

Cues from Export Intensity

Perhaps Cuba's overall economic structure was detrimentally skewed by the embargo. Trade is a key economic activity for small countries and trade restraint is the stated mechanism for economic damage. So comparing Cuba's trade share with that of its non-embargoed neighbours should reveal the purported impact of the embargo. A 2001 report from the Institute for the Integration of Latin America and Caribbean provides raw data from which figure 5 is derived. [28] This source should provide a more complete view than the UN as it dates back to the critical year, 1960, whereas the UN data starts in 1970.

Figure 5: the effect of the embargo on export sector size

Source: derived from *Institute for the Integration of Latin America and Caribbean*, 2001 [29]

For Cuba and its neighbours, the share of exports in GDP was low, near 10%, from 1960 to 1975 (see figure 5 above). The share of exports did not differentiate Cuba from the other islands during the first 15 embargo years. From that time on though, two distinct trends emerged. Jamaica and Puerto Rico continued their rapid rise in export concentration while Dominican Republic and Cuba rose more gradually together. What was the effect on GDP per capita? That question is more complex than it first seems because output and exports are intertwined; they are both causes and effects of each other. So, the outcome is contradictory for the four islands. Jamaica reached a very high export share in GDP (nearly 80% by 1998) while its GDP per capita declined and stagnated. Rising exports did not help raise its output. Puerto Rico's export share was rising at the same time and to the same extent as Jamaica's but its GDP result was the opposite. A steeply rising export share does not ensure growth.

Conversely, Dominican Republic reached a more moderate share of exports in GDP (peaking at 33% in 1997) while its GDP per capita grew steadily. Cuba's export path was the same, but its GDP cycled through stagnation, boom and bust. It seems clear that the trade embargo did not single out Cuba's export share trend, as it was very similar to non-embargoed Dominican Republic. But more importantly, it may not even have had the hidden effect of preventing growth. After all, Jamaica had a high export share and poor GDP growth.

Cuba's total export value peaked in 1986, then gradually declined by 37% over seven years (this and following figures according to UN data). GDP followed this peak and decline, so the share of exports in GDP only fluctuated slightly from 30 to 35% even during the Soviet collapse. One indicative change in exports occurred in 1997, the year following the Helms-Burton embargo tightening when they dropped by a mere 5%. Even so, GDP increased by an enormous 7.8% during the same year as nearly every other sector of the Cuban economy expanded. Its growth ranked third in the Caribbean after only BVI and Turks and Caicos. Again it seems that tightening the embargo may have imposed some extra trade relocation costs and thus squeezed exports, but it did not stifle Cuba's broader economy.

Table 7 (below) shows another export related factor that can help assess the potential embargo impact on Cuba, namely export intensity in GDP. Small countries usually exhibit a greater reliance on trade than larger countries. They often have no domestic source of certain goods such as crude oil and processed metals, so imports provide a ready supply as long as they can be purchased with the proceeds of exports. In this way, exports form a vital link in the small country's economy. Cuba certainly qualifies as a small country and would be expected to show exports as a relatively large proportion of its GDP. If the embargo had a devastating macro impact on Cuba's economy, table 7 would exhibit it as a low export intensity and a correspondingly low GDP per capita.

Table 7: the effect of export intensity on Latin American GDP per capita (2005, in $ current)

	% Exports in GDP	GDP per capita
Brazil	15 %	4,721
Colombia	17 %	3,217
Cuba	21 %	3,787
Guatemala	25 %	2,141
Peru	25 %	2,911
Argentina	25 %	4,728
El Salvador	27 %	2,560
Mexico	27 %	8,096
Dominican Rep.	30 %	3,542
Uruguay	30 %	5,221
Ecuador	31 %	2,847
Nicaragua	33 %	9,55
Bolivia	36 %	1,040
Venezuela	40 %	5,445
Chile	41 %	7,257
Paraguay	51 %	1,266
Costa Rica	57 %	4,614
Honduras	59 %	1,428
Panama	75 %	4,786
(Jamaica	35 %	4,180)
(Puerto Rico	80 %	22,780)

Source: % exports derived from UN National Accounts Database

Table 7 shows that Cuba's export intensity is in the lowest quintile of the Latin American group and by this measure it seems reasonable to conclude that the embargo depressed its export markets. Indeed the Cuban government argues that in the absence of the embargo, Cuba would have done better.

But instead of confirming that low exports resulted in lower economic output, the performance of other countries in the group dispels this likelihood. The main reason is that the top quintile of exporters does not include even one country in the top quintile of output producers. For example, the top exporter, Panama, has a GDP per capita ranking about midway in the group. The next highest exporter, Honduras, has an output level in the bottom quintile. Furthermore, out of these twenty countries, Costa Rica is the third highest exporter, and yet only has the eighth highest output level. In other words, the top ranked exporters have only middling macroeconomic results so export intensity is clearly not crucial for attaining a high GDP per capita.

The data also imply that even if Cuba had higher export intensity, GDP per capita would not likely improve. Honduras had triple the exports as a percentage of GDP and yet its output was 67% less than Cuba's. Brazil had lower export intensity than Cuba and yet had 25% higher output per capita.

Puerto Rico is included in the list in order to extend the ongoing Latin American comparison, and its top ranked output clearly reveals the economic benefit of being fully integrated into the US economy. Cuba's economic isolation is clearly as economically significant as Puerto Rico's integration with the US, but instead of Cuba being devastated it merely ranks midway in output per capita.

A perfect correlation between the percentage of exports in GDP and output per capita would be 1.0, whereas no correlation (i.e. randomness) would be 0.0. In this case the correlation of -0.045 runs counterintuitive to expectations and is very nearly random. For the Latin American group, export intensity in GDP seems to have no association with output per capita and provides no evidence that the embargo constrained Cuba's economic growth.

It may begin to seem that with Cuba's output rank at about midway within the group, no data could possibly show that the embargo had harmed the economy at the macro level. The following hypothetical example presents the kind of evidence that would indicate such harm.

All of the export percentage values (except Cuba's) in table 8 (below) are fabricated for this illustration, whereas the GDP values are true for each country. If Cuba's actual export percentage was in the middle of the field, as is its true GDP per capita, then the correlation would be high and the embargo could be implicated in constraining economic growth. The correlation for this hypothetical but realistic data series is very strong at 0.945, which indicates that a straightforward scenario supporting claims of the embargo's macroeconomic effects could indeed exist.

Table 8: Hypothetical level of 2005 export intensity that would demonstrate embargo harm
(countries are ranked by actual GDP per capita)

	Hypothetical % Exports In GDP	Actual 2005 GDP per capita
Nicaragua	7 %	955
Bolivia	8 %	1,040
Paraguay	9 %	1,266
Honduras	11 %	1,428
Guatemala	15 %	2,141
El Salvador	14 %	2,560
Ecuador	19 %	2,847
Peru	18 %	2,911
Colombia	16 %	3,217
Dominican Rep.	20 %	3,542
Cuba	21 %	3,787
Costa Rica	26 %	4,614
Brazil	45 %	4,721
Argentina	28 %	4,728
Panama	29 %	4,786
Uruguay	47 %	5,221
Venezuela	48 %	5,445
Chile	54 %	7,257
Mexico	59 %	8,096

Source: Actual GDP per capita from UN National Accounts Database, in $2005 current.
Hypothetical % Exports constructed by the author.

The forgoing economic indicators, namely the percentage of exports in GDP and percentage destined to the US, may be seen as merely numerical ratios that can obscure as much as they reveal. High growth from a low level is of little real benefit. In order to ensure that the analysis relates to real output and real exports, figure 6 and table 9 (below) show the total value of exports and their growth in constant dollars. Cuba's rank among Latin American countries and among all countries of the world is then derived.

Figure 6: comparing Cuba's real exports

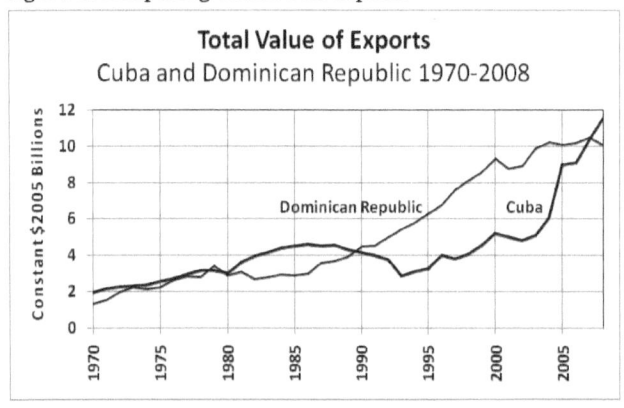

Source: derived from UN National Accounts Database

Cuba's real exports virtually mirrored those of the Dominican Republic at the start and end of the period. Again, the main impact was from the Soviet collapse in the late 1980s. The highest upturns unexpectedly followed the embargo tightening of 1992 and 1996.

Table 9: Growth in Total Real Export Value, Latin American Countries, 1970 - 2008

Average Annual Export Growth

Venezuela	2.1 %
Honduras	2.9 %
Guatemala	3.0 %
Nicaragua	3.9 %
Peru	4.2 %
Bolivia	4.4 %
Cuba	4.8 %
El Salvador	5.0 %
Panama	5.0 %
Dominican Rep.	5.5 %
Argentina	5.6 %
Colombia	5.8 %
Uruguay	6.2 %
Paraguay	6.8 %
Costa Rica	7.2 %
Brazil	7.7 %
Ecuador	7.7 %
Chile	8.0 %
Mexico	8.6 %
Jamaica	1.8 %
Puerto Rico	4.0 %
Canada	4.4 %

Source: derived from UN National Accounts Database in constant $2005

Among the ECLAC 19 Latin American countries, Cuba's export growth ranks seventh from the bottom. Cuba also ranks about half way among the world's exporting countries that have been in existence since 1970 (81st out of 179). New countries that were formed after 1970 such as Uzbekistan are excluded. So Cuba ranks ahead of Bahrain, Canada, UK, Norway, Switzerland, New Zealand, and Monaco, and ninth from the top out of the UN's 21 Caribbean nations.

By any of these measures, Cuba's export growth has been a middling performer in its region and in the world. It might have done better given a free hand in trade, but many more advanced economies also show that it may have done worse. The embargo cannot be interpreted as having been a decisive factor.

One key speculative point regarding exports may bear consideration. According to UN data, Cuba suffered its greatest real loss in exports of about 35% during the Soviet collapse of 1989-93. So what might have happened if the embargo was lifted instead of tightened by the 1992 Torricelli act? In order to be effective, the collapse would have to be recognised and confirmed as such, say within two years of 1989. Then the embargo would have to be lifted and the attendant legal and logistical arrangements settled, say within another year. This implies that Cuba could have started shipments of its uncommitted export goods to the US by 1992, which is about the time that its actual exports reached their nadir. The suggestion is that even lifting the embargo would not likely have made a significant difference given the circumstances. Cuba's exports in fact recovered and did so at a greater pace than most other countries.

The Official Statement on Exports

Cuba's statistical agency, ONE, provides a limited amount of recent historical data online, and this can be used to assess the official claim on export constraint due to the embargo. It can also be compared with other current sources such as the UN. The August 2007 edition of ONE's *Goods Exports Indices, Year 49 of the Revolution* [30], compiles data from 1996 to 2006.

Relative to 1996, the year of Helms-Burton embargo reinforcement, the subsequent three years saw Cuba's index of exports decline by a total of about 20%. Is this the devastation said to be caused by the embargo tightening? This decline can be compared to Canada's exports, for example, to assess its severity. The Cuban export decline is about equal to the combined impact of the 2008 recession and the appreciation of Canada's currency on its highly trade dependent economy (Canada's exports account for about 37% of GDP). The decline in Cuba's exports does not seem to indicate the extent of damage claimed by the government, even disregarding the rapid recovery and substantial further gains listed by the official data set.

The recovery in Cuban exports resulted in a 60% increase over the ten years from 1996 to 2006 according to the same official figures. This amounts to an annual average increase in export value of 4.81%, which at first blush does not seem so low as to suggest an economy under siege. But because this data set cannot be directly compared to that of other countries, UN data will help assess the official Cuban position.

The UN figures for this period show Cuba's exports growing at an even higher annual average rate, 8.5%. This compares outstandingly well with America's export growth of 4.5% or Puerto Rico's at 5.2%, or Dominican Republic's at 4.2% or Jamaica's at virtually zero (all in constant $2005).

In this analysis, regardless of which figures are used, Cuba's export growth matched or exceeded that of its neighbours and the US in the decade following two legislative acts strengthening the supposedly devastating embargo. Although the embargo may have depressed Cuba's export growth for a brief period, it seems difficult not to conclude that its macro impact was quickly undone.

The entire group of Latin American countries provides no evidence that exporting to the US raises the exporter's industrial output and this result casts serious doubt on the idea that Cuba has been deprived of an important economic opportunity.

All four types of export figures reviewed here provide no indication that the embargo has depressed Cuba's economy in aggregate:

- % of exports destined for US
- export intensity in GDP
- export growth trend
- total value of exports

Considering that the embargo bans imports and exports, and that the government claims that it labours under economic warfare, one should expect to see less trade than most other countries, less export growth than most other countries and less export value than most countries of similar size. One should also expect to see most countries that export to the US to have greater output per capita than Cuba. Instead, none of these reasonably expected outcomes exists.

Cuba's report to the UN General Assembly resolutely states that America's legislative changes to the embargo worsened its impact:

> "The 1996 Helms-Burton Act made the effects of the blockade worse, increased the number and scope of the provisions with an extraterritorial impact, instituted persecution of and sanctions on actual and potential foreign investors in Cuba and authorised funding for hostile, subversive and aggressive acts against the Cuban people." [31]

But the effect of US trade cannot be discerned in the data either at the global or regional levels. The short term trend, say two to three years, in the total value of Cuban exports runs counter to the dates of two US embargo reinforcements in the 1990s.

The Impact on Fixed Capital

The UN has also tracked gross fixed capital formation for each country and this can be used to assess the ongoing development of the industrial base through savings, domestic investment, and foreign direct investment. Embargo impacts may be inferred if Cuba stands out from the Latin American group or its Caribbean neighbours.

Table 10 (below) compiles the overall change in annual fixed capital formation for each Latin American country from 1970 to 2008. (For clarity, if capital formation was $1billion in 1970 and $2billion in 2008 the change is shown as 100%.) This indicates the growth of the means of production, infrastructure, buildings and equipment, and the ability of the economy to sustain itself. Corresponding 2005 GDP per capita figures are from the UN online database, as are the original figures on gross fixed capital formation.

Table 10: the relation of Gross Fixed Capital Formation and Latin American GDP per capita (2005, in $ current)

	GDP per capita	Fixed Capital Growth
Cuba	3,787	162 %
Nicaragua	955	201 %
Venezuela	5,445	237 %
Argentina	4,728	262 %
Bolivia	1,040	278 %
Uruguay	5,221	295 %
El Salvador	2,560	345 %
Mexico	8,096	367 %
Brazil	4,721	372 %
Ecuador	2,847	383 %
Guatemala	2,141	412 %
Panama	4,786	523 %
Colombia	3,217	524 %
Honduras	1,428	630 %
Paraguay	1,266	637 %
Chile	7,257	653 %
Peru	2,911	654 %
Costa Rica	4,614	842 %
Dominican Rep.	3,542	859 %
(Jamaica	4,180	135 %)
(Puerto Rico	22,780	179 %)

Source: derived from UN National Accounts Database

Cuba's growth in capital formation ranks last in the Latin American group, possibly signalling the effect of the embargo having prevented the importation of equipment required to modernise the economy. This mechanism is plausible, but can it be related to Cuba's claim that the embargo blocks the financing needed to support its aggregate economic growth?

Although Cuba's capital formation growth rate is lowest among Latin American countries, it ranks slightly higher than Jamaica and barely behind Puerto Rico. Those Caribbean countries were free to import capital goods and yet their rate of capital formation was in the same low range as Cuba's. The embargo did not single out Cuba in this way, so the embargo harm mechanism is less than plausible. Further, Dominican Republic's capital formation grew over five times faster than Cuba's, and yet their GDP per capita ended the period at virtually the same level. Even among the Latin American countries, Cuba under embargo attained the exact middle rank in GDP per capita. Several other countries with equally high capital formation had worse GDP per capita. The embargo seems irrelevant to Cuba's economy by this measure.

It may still be possible, though, that another hidden or unrecognised embargo-related mechanism works to depress Cuba's economy. This idea should be dismissed for two reasons.

First, it is difficult to imagine a factor that remains hidden yet still has a severe macroeconomic impact on Cuba. Cuba's output per capita lies in the middle of the Latin American field even though it alone operates under a wide ranging embargo. If for example, an embargo-induced shortage of foreign direct investment (FDI) was claimed to critically depress Cuba, then the freedom to accept FDI should have lifted other low income Latin American countries. That has not been the case, and of course the same argument works against other similar claims.

Second, and more importantly, Cuba's leadership has full access to all of the relevant national account statistics and is best situated to assess all of the relevant economic factors. The government should be able identify the specific factors and mechanisms contributing to the shortfall in economic performance. Instead Cuba's leaders have repeatedly claimed that the embargo's restraint of trade with the US is the crucial factor working against their progress, and yet even their own published figures show continued robust macroeconomic growth that contradicts their fundamental claim.

A key Cuban export commodity, sugar cane.
Source: Hannes Grobe (public domain)

6 Revealing Industrial Structure

Cuba does not stand out within its region or within the Latin American group when judged by trends in the obvious macroeconomic measures such as GDP per capita or exports. The embargo should have affected Cuba due to its sanctions against the movement of goods and financial capital, although the mechanism by which this is thought to operate may have been subverted by the actions of other sympathetic or opportunistic countries. Another approach may be needed to detect features of Cuba's economy that can differentiate it from other countries and possibly signal the embargo's macro level impact.

Even though no clear effect from the embargo was found in Cuba's export figures, damage to Cuba's long term GDP *potential* might have been done by a different mechanism. In other words, while being in the middle of the GDP pack shows that Cuba has not been crushed, it does not prove that Cuba could not have done better. So the most germane question becomes: if the embargo has had a real macroeconomic impact, is there another kind of indicator that shows Cuba lagging its regional peers or the rest of the world? After all, since Cuba is the only country under US embargo for 50 years, it should also have some key distinguishing economic feature that reflects its unique situation. If not, then the embargo must be in vain.

Long term growth trends around the world don't suggest that more exports lead to more economic growth. Growth trends may, however, suggest another relevant link between a country's exports and its industrial structure: the share of agriculture in GDP. This link can be used as a new instrument to discern embargo effects on Cuba's economy.

How is agriculture relevant to exports? Cuban industrial policy often maintained a bias toward farm commodities that were subject to generally declining world prices. Selling commodities at falling prices reduces export earnings. For decades, Cuba's inefficient farm sector tied up over 25% of its national workforce to generate just 15% of its GDP [32]. Compared to other wealthier countries, fewer workers were available to manufacturing industries producing higher value-added tradable goods that bring higher export earnings. This labour inefficiency also maintains the relatively high cost of food, leaving less income for goods that promote technological progress in the tradable sector (materials, machinery, electrical equipment, etc.). The key is that farm efficiency must rise first in order to free up labour for other sectors. Did the embargo prevent this from happening? In other words, was Cuba mired in low value agriculture more than other non-embargoed countries? Did its shift in agricultural concentration signal a restraint on Cuba's economic growth? This is an entirely new approach to economic investigation.

Throughout the world, more concentration on agriculture means lower economic output in almost every case. All very poor countries derive over 7% of GDP from agriculture. For countries that have between 3% and 7% of GDP in agriculture, economic output on average rises quickly as agriculture fades in relative importance; GDP per capita rises to a moderate level. With even less agriculture, output booms at a startling pace; all very rich countries are at less than 3%.

Figure 7: the embargo's effect on Cuba's industrial structure

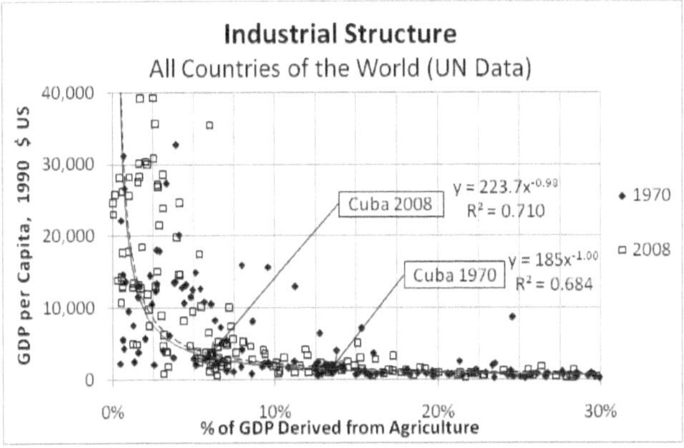

Industrial Structure
All Countries of the World (UN Data)

[Scatter plot showing GDP per Capita (1990 $ US) on y-axis from 0 to 40,000 versus % of GDP Derived from Agriculture on x-axis from 0% to 30%. Trendlines shown:
- Cuba 2008: $y = 223.7x^{-0.93}$, $R^2 = 0.710$
- Cuba 1970: $y = 185x^{-1.00}$, $R^2 = 0.684$
Data series marked ♦ 1970 and □ 2008]

Source: derived from UN National Accounts Database

At the beginning and end of the UN data series, Cuba's economic output remained exactly on a par with countries of similar structure. Figure 7 shows that in 2008, Cuba produced $3,547 of output per capita and 6.1% of GDP from agriculture.

Figure 7 also provides two signals about Cuba's industrial progress: its current level and its shift over time. The world's level of agriculture in GDP was 5.0% in 2008 whereas Cuba's was very close at 6.1%. But since 1970, the world's agricultural share had dropped by 1.7% whereas Cuba's had progressed far more rapidly, dropping by 7.4%.

This global aggregate data shows that Cuba made definite progress in its industrial transition. This finding can be confirmed by another measure: a simple average of each country's percentage shift (instead of the shift in the aggregate). The world average shift in agricultural concentration was a decline of 5.8%. As with many moderately developed economies from 1970 to 2008, Cuban agriculture's share in GDP declined from 13.5% to 6.1% of GDP, as its manufacturing and services sectors grew. This decline of 7.4% shows Cuba's industrial transition progressing at a somewhat higher rate than the world average, again indicating that the embargo was economically ineffective.

In 1970, the world trend line relating GDP per capita to its agricultural concentration was given by the following equation:

GDPpc = 185.0(agrishare)$^{-1.00}$

This says that with 13.5% of GDP in agriculture, Cuba would be expected to have $1370 in output per person if it conformed to the world's trend. Cuba's actual output was $1441, meaning that Cuba was at 5% higher output than expected of countries with the same industrial structure.

In 2008, the world average equation was

GDPpc = $223.7(\text{agrishare})^{-0.98}$

So Cuba's 6.1% of GDP in agriculture yields an expected output of $3468 per capita, whereas its actual output was $3547. Again, after nearly 40 years of embargo, Cuba was at 2.5% higher output than countries of similar structure.

Cuba's industrial transition can be contrasted with two outlier countries, Iceland and Botswana. In 2008 Iceland had a very high output per capita of $34,545, a level which is usually accompanied by very low agriculture, about 2%. Why does Iceland have triple that amount, 6% of GDP in agriculture? Its outlier status seems to be related to its heavy reliance on fishing, which is included in the agricultural sector as a standard practice in the system of national accounts.

With a very low concentration on agriculture, 1.6%, Botswana would be expected to have a very high GDP per capita if it conformed to the world trend. Instead its output is $4932, less than one half of the trend level. Although this output level is lower than most countries of this industrial structure, Botswana's economy is in rapid positive transition partly due to a shift from farming to diamond mining. In this case, industrial structure changed first and GDP is now catching up. It may not be an outlier for long.

Like Iceland, Botswana has made its advance based on specialisation and a relatively free market system. Iceland's fishing and Botswana's mining can explain their deviation from the world trend line. It is reasonable to expect that Cuba's embargo should be at least as impactful as the mundane market factors that shift entire economies in other countries. If the embargo was economically impactful, Cuba should exhibit a similar deviation from the world trend in figure 7 but that is clearly not the case. Instead, Cuba's level of agriculture as well as its long term trend kept a very close pace with the global structural shift for decades.

Gravity and Industrial Structure

CubavsBlockade, billing itself as the 'Cuban People Website' [sic], claims that transport costs are among the embargo's most serious causes of economic loss:

> "Among the elements that most seriously affect Cuban exports are the cost of maritime transportation (freight); insurance premiums on cargo and transportation; the increase in risks and damage to merchandise owing to the distance it must travel..." [33]

Transportation has often been viewed as an important cost in global trade, even though it was rendered insignificant by the introduction of steamships in the 19th century. Shipping costs were pushed so low as to allow Argentine beef and wheat exports to transform European farming. New Zealand's agricultural products started to be sold half a world away.

Today, China's largest export market is the US and shipping costs have been a negligible factor. Likewise, Cuba should be far less impacted by shipping costs than it may first seem. The Cuban claim of serious impact does not square well with historical and current global trends in transport technology.

The Gravity Theory of Trade can help explain why the selection of trading partners is not as simple as identifying large nearby markets.

A large economy is expected to exert a tremendous influence on a nearby small economy, whereas the small one will merely exert a weak influence in return. As a result, trade flows could tend to drive the structure of the smaller economy to more closely resemble the larger one. Personal and financial contacts would establish business confidence while trading agreements and experience with customs simplify technology transfers to the smaller economy. Some economists conversely believe that the smaller country would develop a different industrial structure due to specialisation, although two examples in the North American and European regions do not support this view.

In this specialisation based view, Canada, for example, would specialise its exports, perhaps in agricultural products, and so end up with a very distinct industrial structure relative to the US. Instead, Canada's small economy, deeply reliant on trade with the US, has a nearly indistinguishable economic structure. Agriculture contributes a small share of GDP, and output per capita is high in both countries. But Canada has no large nearby trading alternative, so another example could help to establish a pattern (Russia is Canada's other cross-border neighbour, but with its trans-polar location is obviously not geographically equivalent to the US).

Finland presents another example that refutes the belief in structural divergence due to gravity. Finland's situation resembles the Caribbean, a small economy located between two enormous nearby economies. Russia and Germany are Finland's largest regional neighbours and trading partners. Here, gravity theory presents conflicting signals in that trade with Germany should be stronger due to its large GDP, but slightly weaker due to its marginally greater distance. The outcome is that Finland's trade is nearly equal between its two largest neighbours, so gravity theory fares well on that account. Moreover, since the distances involved are at a similar scale, Finland's industrial structure has a stronger resemblance to Germany's far larger economy than to Russia's.

Finland's structure has also turned out to be virtually identical to Sweden, its smaller cross-border neighbour with which it shares deep linguistic and historic roots. Both small countries have over double the agricultural share and 40% higher GDP per capita than Germany. This result suggests that gravity theory can predict industrial structure based on culture as well as geographic factors.

The geographic distance aspect of gravity theory predicts that the Caribbean receives an equal influence from North and South America owing to its position about midway between the continents. The small scale island economies such as Cuba should benefit from opportunities to specialise and transport goods just as easily in either direction, north or south. However, the vastly larger American economy should be the dominant influence and bias the islands' GDP per capita higher than South America's, even though the islands share a deep cultural connection with the southern continent. This reflects the idea of the US being Cuba's so-called *natural market*, and suggests that the Caribbean's structure should resemble North America more than South America. So in figure 8 (below) the Caribbean point should lie closer to North America than South America.

Figure 8: comparing industrial structure of the Caribbean

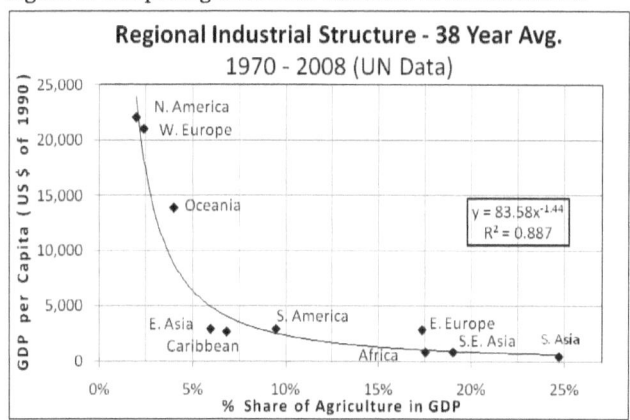

Source: derived from UN National Accounts Database

The expected result has clearly not occurred, as figure 8 shows the Caribbean's output level and structure to closely resemble South America's. The simple and obvious implication is that cultural affinity plays a much stronger role than geo-economic factors of GDP scale and physical distance. In effect, it may also imply that the US may not be Cuba's supposed 'natural market'. This idea can be further tested by examining another isolated island group, Oceania.

Oceania includes most of the small South Pacific island nations but is economically dominated by Australia and, secondarily, by New Zealand. These island economies are geographically isolated from their Western, English speaking founders and should bear a strong economic disadvantage due to relatively high shipping costs for their traded goods. Trade relations should rather tend to favour nearby economic giants and as a result, Australia's industrial structure might not be expected to evolve to resemble Europe's.

Southeast Asia, being the physically adjacent economic group and the world's fourth most populous region, might also have biased Australia's structure away from Europe's, but neither of these expectations have materialised. Instead, Oceania lies at the *opposite* end of the graph from Southeast Asia in figure 8. Australia's industrial structure does not most closely resemble China or Indonesia. Instead, it resembles the largest economy that shares its cultural background regardless of distance, namely the UK and Western Europe. Again, it seems that the obvious cultural affinity of Australia and Western Europe has outweighed the geo-economic factors.

Gravity theory answers this unexpected outcome by evolving the naive concept of physical distance into 'economic distance', which combines all barriers to trade. So economic distance includes transport costs, tariffs, language barriers, traditional preferences, corruption, colonial history, and the like. Furthermore, multiple countries can interact and affect the trade between a single pair of countries. For a simple example, one country within a region uses a unique language and maintains strict product label regulations, so more trade will tend to flow between the other countries. This recognition has led to the view that trade is much more influenced by multilateral barriers than by physical distance.

Since gravity theory focuses on trade, it has yet to address the subject of industrial structure that might shed light on Cuba's economic performance. The current search for evidence of the embargo's macro impact introduces structure as new element to the gravity theory.

Figure 8 demonstrates a clear non-linear relation of economic output to industrial structure; at less than 3% agriculture in GDP, output rises rapidly. The two major island groups, Oceania and Caribbean, also indicate a strong association between industrial structure and culture. That is to say, gravity between countries that share a culture makes those countries structurally similar.

So Oceania's industrial structure is related to its historic association with Western Europe, and more likely due to its cultural affinity than any geographic factor found in the gravity theory. Fully one half of Australia's bilateral trade is with OECD countries, [34] which at first seems strange given that the OECD group is geographically the most distant. Although this fact points to the later discovery that cultural factors also determine trade volume, it may suggest a more significant link, namely the effect of culture on industrial structure.

Likewise, the Caribbean's structure gravitates toward South America rather than North America because of its much longer historic association. These findings do not work to refute the gravity theory of trade, as it currently does not address industrial structure. But they indicate another promising layer in the geo-economic analysis of Cuba under embargo. It now seems likely that in the absence of the embargo, Cuba would have ended up exactly where it is today, structurally more similar to Latin America than the US. Puerto Rico shows that full economic integration with the US is the most likely feature in its divergence from South America's industrial structure.

In the Caribbean, the largest economies are primarily Spanish speaking and as a group, their structure closely resembles Spanish speaking Latin America. This situation might seem inconsistent due to a significant exception, English speaking Jamaica. Nevertheless modern gravity theory would point to Jamaica's Spanish origins and conclude that its structural resemblance to Latin American is unsurprising. Cultural connections are thought to be extremely persistent, their effects lingering for centuries. [35] In Puerto Rico's case, its full economic integration with the US renders it irrelevant to this issue because it functions as a US state instead of a trading nation.

The effects of culture, broadly defined to include historical connections, may help to explain why trading with the US is not strongly correlated with increased economic output, and why the embargo is less relevant to Cuba's trade sector than it naively appears at first blush.

Cuba and Gravity Today

Cuba's largest export destination countries by total value in 2006 were as follows (officially quoted at an unspecified currency base year):

        Netherlands   773,621,000 p
        Canada   546,075,000 p
        Venezuela   296,187,000 p
        China   245,744,000 p

Source: Oficina Nacional de Estadisticas
www.one.cu/aec2006/anuariopdf2006/capitulo7/VII.5.pdf

In 2001, 66% of Cuba's exports went to Europe. By 2006 this had shifted to 45 % of its exports going to over 26 European countries. Of the remainder, 41% went to the Americas and 14% to Asia. Official data show that Cuba ships its goods to all continents and to most countries of the world, so its export activity hardly seems constrained by distance. Instead it seems that the net effect of favourable international trade policies has been to Cuba's economic benefit. Through decades of embargo, countries around the world have voted with Cuba at the UN to end the sanctions but have also taken practical trade actions to ease Cuba's path. As unilateral barriers to US trade were erected, the overall effect was that multi-lateral barriers became relatively diminished; Cuba gravitated toward the rest of the world.

The official data show that its largest trading partner in 2006 was the Netherlands, which is a major ocean farther than the US. While transport and insurance costs are undoubtedly higher than they would have been for exporting to the US, the question at hand remains whether or not such costs or other export constraints were crippling to the extent that they constituted a serious effect on Cuban exports, or indeed economic warfare. A great deal of focus is cast on the Helms-Burton extraterritorial provisions of the embargo and their stifling effect on trade. Judging by the officially documented extensive list of countries that trade with Cuba, such constraint has not significantly materialised.

Moreover, trade with Canada can be used as a proxy for the threat level perceived by Cuba's potential trading partners. Canada's trade is vastly concentrated on the US, and, on this basis alone, trading with Cuba poses a great risk of American retaliation against Canada. But, instead of shying away from Cuban trade, Canada has defied the US edict by legally prohibiting its domestic firms from complying with Helms-Burton provisions.[36] As a result, Canada ranks as Cuba's second largest export destination. In this instance, the embargo has not only failed to inhibit Cuban trade, it may in fact have greatly stimulated that trade.

From a geographic perspective, Cuba's distance from Canada is similar to its distance from much of the US. A major nearby market had developed to fill the embargo void. Meanwhile, yet another transition favourable to Cuba had occurred; Venezuela had assumed the former USSR's role as Cuba's crude oil supplier. The source of Cuba's most significant import commodity would now be in the immediate neighbourhood instead of half a world away. Transport costs would correspondingly fall, but again, Cuba's government lists the losses from the embargo and not the gains from sympathising countries that act to negate its effects.

Furthermore, as Cuba's structure shifted more intensively toward the services export sector, transport costs become less relevant. For example, Cuba's distance from three out of four major tourism markets is identical to that of other Caribbean islands. These markets are Europe, Canada, and South America. In this regard, it suffers no disadvantage, implying that the government claims of great economic losses due to transport costs are becoming even less relevant. The denial of the fourth major tourism market (America) is undoubtedly a significant aspect of the embargo, although again, this is only part of the picture.

It is fairly straightforward to claim what benefits would have accrued to Cuba's tourism sector without the embargo, but it is also informative to recognise what actually happened. The Caribbean is practically the only winter vacation destination for the Southern Cone countries, Argentina, Uruguay and Chile, which gives Cuba a language advantage as well as the potential for political sympathy due to the embargo. But while other Caribbean countries built their tourism industry and shifted further toward financial services in the 1970s and 1980s, Cuba's economic policy continued its focus on sugar and mining. Success in developing a tourism industry relies exclusively on the Cuban government's policies, which seem to have been late in coming and incremental in their pace. The result is that while American tourists were barred, Cuba's opportunity to fill the gap went unheeded by its own choice.

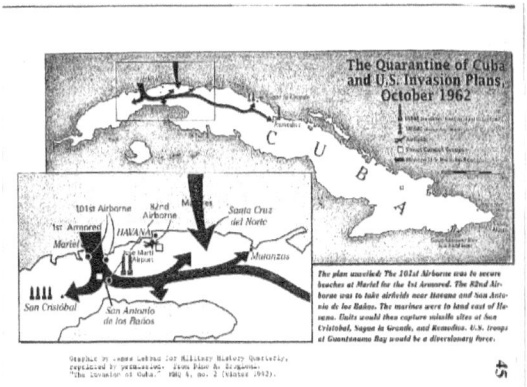

Military History Quarterly, US invasion plan, 1962.
Source: © The National Security Archive, GWU.

Ship reloading missiles, Casilda, Cuba, Nov. 6, 1962.
Source: © The National Security Archive, GWU.

7 Human Development in Cuba

The UN Human Development Index (HDI) has earned broad acceptance as a general composite indicator of the quality of life. Stemming from the conceptual work of economist Mahbub-al-Haq and the economist-philosopher Nobel laureate Amartya Sen, it seeks to provide a more direct and complete numerical measure of well being than is possible to glean from economic income alone. As a final test of the embargo's impact on Cuba, the HDI may reveal trends in the population's well being that a narrow focus on income might obscure.

Gross National Income (GNI) as a measure of human well being suffers from the averaging effect in that it cannot discern the breadth of its benefits. Average income figures may hide intense inequalities that result in widespread poor health. For instance, most of the income in a wealthy country may flow to a small minority while the majority endure malnutrition and a shortened lifespan.

One solution the averaging problem is to add a second indicator, one that quantifies the distribution of income. On a scale of 0 to 1, the Gini coefficient is a single number showing how uniformly a country's income is spread throughout its population. The lowest score indicates that every person has the same income while the highest score indicates that a single person has all of the country's income. In other words, the extremes are perfect equality and perfect inequality. While combining GNI with the Gini coefficient presents a more complete picture, it also complicates the interpretation. If one of these indicators rises slightly as the other declines, is the country better off on the whole? Al-Haq and Sen insisted that a better single indicator was still needed.

Although income has always been recognised as an important element of human well being, it remains a mere enabler of wellness as opposed to an aim or a goal. People cannot eat their income. Rather, they can use it as a means to obtain nourishment, shelter, and education for their families as they aim for long and productive lives. It is the availability of those resources along with real outcomes that matter most so, to that end, HDI combines life expectancy, literacy, and income. And it does so without the disadvantage of averaging that occurs when looking at income alone. That is to say, average income can hide vast disparities while average lifespan cannot. For example, a small minority could have all of a country's income but it cannot have all of the lifespan. Average literacy, lifespan, and years of education will usually be a more accurate reflection of broad based outcomes than average income alone.

For Cuba, the Human Development Index serves as an antidote to the data problem. While it accounts for the purely economic effects of income, it also shows the sufficiency of that income to supporting the ultimate social goals of a long and productive life. So if the embargo has hobbled Cuba's economy and its people's welfare, the HDI should reflect it at least to some minimal extent. The HDI record should confirm or refute Foreign Minister Rodríguez-Parrilla's statement that the embargo has been the prime obstacle to both economic and social growth in Cuba.

The HDI numerical index ranges from 0 to 1, and has traditionally been divided into three general categories:

High:	0.800 to 1.000
Medium:	0.501 to 0.799
Low:	0.000 to 0.500

The UN compiled Cuba's HDI score and ranking among countries of the world as far back as 1985. With this data set, the HDI can be used to assess Cuba's overall economic and social condition along with its progress, and thereby test the embargo's economic effect.

The HDI certainly has been criticised through its evolution over many years, primarily for adding the allegedly redundant measures of life expectancy and literacy onto the previously preferred income indicator, Gross National Income. Some economists point to the inherent strong correlation between the HDI level and the national income level as proof of this redundancy. After all, the HDI is partly composed of income so there must be a certain extent of auto-correlation. (Note that there is little or no correlation between *growth* in income and *growth* in HDI. Rather, the strong correlation is between the income level and the HDI level. Countries with high income overwhelmingly have high HDI.) Others criticise it for generating several glaring aberrations, including Hong Kong and Brazil, in which higher income countries with deep inequality nevertheless score high on the HDI scale. Moreover, literacy rates or years of education can be dubious indicators where education consists, for example, of orthodox indoctrination (such as state propaganda). A multi university system is apt to provide a vastly different benefit from a single state run institution, but the HDI cannot capture that effect.

Regardless of periodic criticism, HDI remains very widely used and provides an evidence based foundation for national comparisons. Recent changes to HDI methodology include a new Very High category, a shift in one of the core measures (from adult literacy to years of schooling), as well as several new concepts and mathematical revisions that do not permit easy comparisons with reports from past years. The most reliable comparisons are presented in recent HDI reports where the UN has recalculated previous data using current methods to ensure compatibility.

For 2011, Cuba's HDI of 0.776 lies in the High Human Development category, and ranks 51st in the UN's world of 187 countries. As an initial comparator, neighbouring Dominican Republic scores 0.689, in the Medium Human Development category, and ranks nearly twice as far down in the world list at 98th. As table 11 shows, both have been rising steadily almost as long as the data have been tracked (since 1985 for Cuba; earlier for others). The only exception was a brief decline in 1995 after the Soviet collapse.

Table 11: Progress in Cuba's HDI

	Cuba	Dominican Republic
1985	.665	.549
1990	.677	.577
1995	.646	.608
2000	.681	.640
2005	.725	.658
2010	.773	.686

See notes for sources [37].

Cuba started the period with a moderate HDI level of 0.665. Meanwhile, Dominican Republic began somewhat lagging at 0.549 even without being under embargo and operating in a generally improving political climate that included a return to democracy. Furthermore, Cuba has maintained its lead throughout the entire period. (Note that Cuba was initially excluded in the 2010 list of countries as it did not provide national income data in the standard format required for comparison and ranking; this was updated after Cuba's official objection). Among Latin American countries, Cuba currently ranks only behind Chile, Argentina, and Uruguay. Cuba also ranks above average within the High Human Development group.

The UN's Human Development Index was nonexistent as of 1960, at the onset of the embargo. This means that a strict comparison of Cuba and other countries cannot be made over the entire embargo period, but several elements of the HDI are available for 1960 as shown in table 12 below. These indicators are the non-economic elements.

Table 12: Elements of Cuba's HDI in recent decades

	1960	1990	2010
Life expectancy	63.8	75.4	79.1
Rank in Latin America	4	1	2
Mortality/1000 under 5 yrs	87	17	6
Rank in Latin America	3	2	1
Mortality/1000 under 1 yr	65	14	5
Rank in Latin America	3	1	1
Adult literacy %	87	95	99.8
Rank in Latin America	5	2	1
School enrolment %	76	95	-
Rank in Latin America	5	2	-
HDI	-	.711	.773
Rank in Latin America	-	10	4
Rank in the world	-	75	51

Source: UN Development Programme, Human Development Report 1990, 1992.

All of the non-economic HDI related indicators listed in table 12 show Cuba as ranking near the peak of the Latin American field in 1960. Furthermore, Cuba's rank among these non-embargoed countries improved from 1960 to 1990 in each of the five measures (infant mortality etc).

What about Cuba's rate of progress in HDI? Even though Cuba ranks well in its regional peer group, has the embargo slowed Cuba's Human Development compared to other non-embargoed countries? Two key comparisons can help to understand the rate of change in HDI: those are the rate of change within the region and within the entire world. If Cuba's HDI growth has lagged, then there may be reason to infer an impact from the embargo. The UN's 2011 HDI Report provides average annual growth rates for all countries and regions. It also lists HDI growth rates for each general category from Very High to Low Human Development.

The record shows that Cuba has virtually matched or exceeded its regional peers in the HDI growth rate for all of the non-economic comparators through the two decades of available data (see table 13). Moreover, not only has Cuba surpassed its regional average and the world's average in the most recent decade, but it has nearly doubled the regional and world HDI growth rates (1.19 % versus 0.66 %).

Table 13: Average Annual Growth rate of HDI

	1990 - 2011	2000 - 2011
Cuba	0.65 %	1.19 %
Lat. Am. & Caribbean	0.76 %	0.66 %
World	0.66 %	0.66 %
High HDI Group	0.64 %	0.70 %

Source: UN Development Programme, Human Development Report 2011

As with economic growth, the Human Development growth rate tends to cluster according to its level. The relation between the level of development and the growth rate is inverse. For example, high income economies such as the US and Japan tend to have lower growth rates than low income economies such as Brazil. As an analogy, where there is more room to grow, the growth rate is higher. Likewise, countries with lower levels of Human Development tend to have faster HDI growth. For this reason, comparisons are usually made between countries in the same category. So in Cuba's case, it is compared with countries in the High HDI category. And in this comparison, not only does its HDI growth seem to have gone unimpeded in the last decade, but Cuba's growth rate is highest in the High Human Development group. Cuba has once again turned out a counterintuitive result: that the US embargo has not impeded its HDI growth.

Among all countries of the world, the truly economically devastated show a very low and declining HDI level. Liberia, Zimbabwe, and Democratic Republic of the Congo have been skidding for decades with HDI levels at less than one half of Cuba's level and only recent tentative recovery. Liberia's literacy rate is a mere 60% of Cuba's while life expectancy barely reaches 57 years compared to 79 in Cuba. Most devastating for Liberia, however, might be its nearly nonexistent per capita income of $265 per year. This amounts to less than one dollar per day and less than one twentieth of Cuba's income.

Cuba's economic situation shares none of the dire qualities exhibited by Liberia; nor do its Human Development indicators. According to its own data, Cuba shows no mass poverty, illiteracy, or high infant mortality. Contrary to the statements of its First Deputy Foreign Minister, and, by its own publicised documents, Cuba's economy maintains brisk growth while its population has enjoyed good health outcomes that continue to improve over the long term. After fifty years of embargo, Cuba simply doesn't appear to be suffering economic devastation or externally imposed obstacles to economic and social growth.

The general conclusion from the UN's Human Development data must be that the embargo has had little impact. Claims of grave, widespread economic and social impacts require corroborating data at the macro level, exactly like the HDI. But the HDI data show the exact opposite of the Cuban government's claims. Furthermore, the raw data used by the UN to generate the index originate with each national government. In other words, Cuba's government provides the raw data that shows its high world ranking as well as brisk progress in Human Development, even while it claims to have ruinous external obstacles to social growth.

Although the Cuban authorities may gain some international prestige from a high HDI level they also forfeit the strength of their claims to being harmed by the embargo. After all, the higher the level of Cuba's Human Development Index, the higher must be Cuba's combination of income and non-economic standard of living.

Confrontation at the UN, Oct. 25, 1962. American and Soviet Ambassadors Adlai Stevenson and Valerian Zorin.
Source: © The National Security Archive, GWU.

Bruno Rodriguez-Parílla at the United Nations.
Source: E. Dusepo (public domain).

8 The Macro Impact

Data from every source indicate the embargo's macroeconomic irrelevance to Cuba. The embargo did not interrupt growth in GDP per capita, trade volumes remained within their usual range, and the economy's structural transition was indistinguishable from the world trend.

The timing of Cuba's 1990s economic contraction had no relation to embargo tightening dates. The US Helms-Burton Act and the entire embargo definitely had an impact on the location of trade, which was diverted from west to east and back again, but any macroeconomic impact did not materialise. Indeed every comparative measure at every geographic scale from local to global confirms that the embargo's net economic effect was virtually zero.

Is the idea of an ineffective embargo really a radical one? Is it even possible that the US embargo against a small island nation like Cuba has no macroeconomic impact? Three public documents show that it is not only possible, but also entirely commonplace in a world of experience.

A major study by the Peterson Institute shows that the percentage of cases in which embargoes fail is quite high. [38] Among all cases of economic of sanctions from World War 2 until 1999, 69% failed to achieve their stated goals. Among unilateral US economic sanctions in the same period, 75% failed. Confirming the Peterson conclusion, Swedish economist Lundborg finds that sanctions are already well known to fail:

> "Although most sanctions have been considered failures, the US has continued to use them...when military action has been judged too dangerous." [39]

Second, a study by the US General Accounting Office reaffirms that embargoes usually do not have the intended impact, and proposed an economic mechanism for their failure:

> "Economic sanctions can raise the cost of trade and finance to the targeted nations, but in most cases have not ruined their economies. Actual damage rarely compares with the threatened pain because of the illicit evasion of sanctions and the legal redirection of the target's trade and financial flows." [40]

Third, the aforementioned US International Trade Commission reported to the House of Representatives about the embargo's weak impact on Cuba's economy. Although it may seem that America would welcome a finding of robust efficacy after decades of effort, the report concluded that the embargo has instead had little effect. The commission, in fact, found the negative impact on America's own business firms to be greater.

How could a policy of such intense focus by the world's largest industrial economy fail to be economically effective against a miniscule adversary? The mechanisms are straightforward and mundane. The first order response to a trade sanction is simply to start trading with other countries, and Cuba did just that. The US accounted for about 60% of Cuba's sugar exports before the revolution, after which the Soviet Union's new purchases rose from virtually nil to 75% within just two years. [41]

Not only did the USSR totally counteract the loss of Cuba's American sugar market in shipped volume, but the price they paid ranged from comparable to astronomical. The US economist J.F. Pérez-López reports that Cuba received up to seven times the price for its sugar exports that the USSR paid to other countries. So in addition to finding replacement markets, the embargo attracted significant new subsidies or revenues to Cuba. Furthermore, there is some suggestion that Cuba purchased crude oil from the Soviet Union at heavily discounted prices, and then resold it at higher world market prices for a net gain. Such actions would have increased Cuba's GDP and further helped to offset the embargo's negative economic effects. They also help to explain how unilateral trade sanctions continue to be easily subverted.

Some Cuban allies such as Canada and the United Kingdom, who enacted legislation that banned compliance with the American Helms-Burton Act of 1996, also intentionally subverted the US embargo. These countries, regardless of their simultaneously being US allies, required their domestic firms to disregard the US bill and provided financial and legal support to those firms that did so. The international community remains steadfastly opposed to the embargo, voting overwhelmingly in support of annual UN resolutions to abandon it while backstopping those votes with legal action.

A number of US tourists who are sympathetic to Cuba (or simply opposed to the embargo on moral or economic grounds) find ways to evade the travel restrictions such as transiting through third countries. Tourism is simply a form of exported services, and subversive tourism adds further to the Cuban GDP. Cuban-Americans also legally remit US cash to their families in Cuba, which yet again increases the country's GDP and provides a source of hard currency that in effect augments export earnings.

With trade substitution, politically motivated international subsidies, subversion and remittances, it is no surprise that the US embargo did not result in a net negative impact on the Cuban macro economy. It undoubtedly had sectoral effects as well as creating additional drag on the government's managerial efficiency. But if the observer's focus is trained away from the impact on specific economic sectors, the embargo's incapacity is not a radical notion. Until now the embargo merely hasn't been analysed at a macro level that includes offsetting actions and comparisons with the relevant international actors.

Appendix 1: Embargo Timeline

1917   US passes Trading With the Enemy Act (Cuba is the only country still affected)

1959   US recognises Castro's new government. Cuba expropriates foreign owned assets.

1960   US revokes Cuba's sugar quota on July 6. US bans exports to Cuba except food and medicines in October.

1961   US suspends diplomatic relations with Cuba on January 3.
US invades Cuba at Bay of Pigs in April.
US passes Foreign Assistance Act in September, authorising the president to impose a trade embargo on Cuba.
December 2 Castro declares himself a Marxist-Leninist.

1962   US bans Cuban imports in February. US suspends Cuba's preferential trade treatment and most favoured nation status in May.

USSR builds nuclear missile bases in Cuba. US quarantines Cuba and resolves dispute in November.

1963 US freezes Cuban assets in the US and regulates transactions by American citizens (July).
Cuba gets long term contract to sell sugar to USSR and receives USSR aid.

1964 Cuban arms found in Venezuela. OAS applies economic sanctions against Cuba in July.

1975 OAS repeals Cuba sanctions in July.
US allows US foreign subsidiaries to trade with Cuba.
Cuba sends combat troops to Angola.

1978 US allows remittances to families in Cuba in January.
Cuba sends combat troops to Ethiopia.

1978 Soviet combat brigade observed in Cuba.

1980 First Cuban refugees arrive in US by boat.

1985 Cuba reported as trading world sugar to USSR for oil at subsidised prices to gain foreign exchange.

1986 US reduces family remittance limits.

1989   USSR economic collapse begins.

1991   Cuba withdraws troops from Angola.
       USSR withdraws troops from Cuba.
       USSR ends subsidies to Cuba in December.

1992   US passes Cuban Democracy Act CDA
       (Torricelli Bill) in October, banning US
       foreign subsidiaries from Cuban trade, and
       food and medicine trade not directed to the
       Cuban people.
       Canada, UK ban CDA compliance.
       Russia and Cuba resume sugar for oil trade
       at greatly reduced levels.
       UN votes to urge an end to the embargo.

1995   Cuban air force shoots down a private US
       plane flown by anti-Castro refugee group.

1996   US passes Cuban Liberty and Democratic
       Solidarity (Libertad) Act (Helms-Burton
       Act) in March, extending the embargo to
       foreign companies trading with Cuba.
       EU, Canada and Mexico ban compliance
       with Libertad Act.
       Hurricane Lili hits Cuba.

1998   US and EU resolve a dispute about
       Helms-Burton in May.

2000	US passes Trade Sanctions Reform and Export Enhancement Act in October, allowing trade in food and medicines but banning finance for this trade. Ongoing US presidential waivers of the Libertad Act.
2005	Hurricanes Dennis and Wilma hit Cuba, causing $2 billion in damage. 2006 15th consecutive vote by the UN to urge an end to the US embargo.
2008	Raul Castro assumes official power in Cuba. EU lifts diplomatic sanctions against Cuba.
2009	US eases most family travel and remittance restrictions to Cuba.

Sources: US International Trade Commission; Case Studies in Economic Sanctions and Terrorism (60-3), 2011, Peterson Institute for International Economics.

Appendix 2: Web Link Resources

US Office of Foreign Assets Control, Dept. of the Treasury
www.treasury.gov/about/organizational-structure/offices/Pages/Office-of-Foreign-Assets-Control.aspx

US Department of the Treasury, Cuba Sanctions
www.treasury.gov/resource-center/sanctions/Programs/Pages/cuba.aspx

Historical documents on foreign relations after the Cuban revolution from the US Office of the Historian, Dept. of State
http://history.state.gov/historicaldocuments/frus1961-63v10/comp1

Cuban people web site [sic]
www.cubavsbloqueo.cu

Historical timeline during the Kennedy presidency (1961-3) from the Cuba vs. Blockade website
www.cubavsbloqueo.cu/Default.aspx?tabid=749

Timelines for other presidents from the same site
www.cubavsbloqueo.cu/Default.aspx?tabid=96

The Official newspaper of the Cuban Government
www.granma.cu/ingles/

Cuba's embassy in Canada
www.cubadiplomatica.cu/canada/EN/Blockade.aspx

The National Security Archive at George Washington University
www.gwu.edu/~nsarchiv/nsa/terms.htm

Official CV of the First Deputy Foreign Minister
www.cubaminrex.cu/English/ministry/Curriculum_ministro.htm

Sample yearbooks from Cuba's statistical office
www.one.cu/aec2005.htm
www.one.cu/aec2009/esp/08_tabla_cuadro.htm

Economic Commission for Latin America and Caribbean (ECLAC)
www.eclac.org/default.asp?idioma=IN

Inter-American Development Bank, The Institute for the Integration of Latin America and the Caribbean
www.iadb.org/en/intal/intal-home,1081.html

Cuban Research Institute at the Florida International University
casgroup.fiu.edu/cri/

Cambridge University's Journal of Latin American Studies
journals.cambridge.org/action/displayJournal?jid=LAS

London University's International Journal of Cuban Studies
cubanstudies.plutojournals.org/

United Nations National Accounts Main Aggregates Database
unstats.un.org/unsd/snaama/dnlList.asp

OECD Statistics
www.oecd-ilibrary.org/statistics

Groningen University Growth and Development Centre, including the Maddison Databases
www.rug.nl/feb/Onderzoek/Onderzoekscentra/GGDC/databases

Penn World Table, Center for International Comparison
pwt.econ.upenn.edu/php_site/pwt_index.php

Council On Foreign Relations
www.cfr.org/region/cuba/ri213

U.S. - Cuba Trade and Economic Council, Inc.
www.cubatrade.org/

Amnesty International's Page on the Cuba Embargo
www.amnesty.org/en/library/info/AMR25/007/2009

Cato Institute's Page on the Cuba Embargo
www.cato.org/publications/speeches/four-decades-failure-us-embargo-against-cuba

An Article from The Economist on the Cuba Embargo
www.economist.com/node/11920925

Wikipedia's Cuba Embargo Page
en.wikipedia.org/wiki/United_States_embargo_against_Cuba

A variety of information on Cuba
www.cubasource.org

A Cuba Embargo Timeline
www.historyofcuba.com/history/funfacts/embargo.htm

Appendix 3: Reading List

Academic Papers and Other Documents

Does Agriculture Really Matter For Economic Growth In Developing Countries?
2009, Titus O. Awokuse

Cuba On The Eve Of The Socialist Transition. 1998, Eric N. Baklanoff

Why America Should Lift Its Cuban Embargo 1994, Ruben Berrios

The Miracle Of The Cuban Economy In The 1990s.
2001, Ed Canler

Latin American Economic Development: 1950-1980
1989, Eliana Cardoso and Albert Fishlow

Report From Havana: Time For A Reality Check On US Policy Toward Cuba
2001, Jonathan Clarke and William Ratliff

Changes In Sectoral Composition Associated With Economic Growth
1997, Cristina Echevarria

The Economic Impact Of U.S. Sanctions With Respect To Cuba
2001, Jonathan R. Coleman

Bill No.: H.R. 796; 107th Congress. United States International Trade Commission Washington, DC 20436
Memorandum To The Committee On Ways And Means Of The United States House Of Representatives On Proposed Tariff Legislation. 2002

Renaissance And Decay: A Comparison Of Socioeconomic Indicators In Pre-Castro And Current-Day Cuba
1998, Kirby Smith and Hugo Llorens

Cuba: Economic Growth And International Linkages - Challenges For Measurement And Vulnerabilities In A Bimonetary Economy
2009, Gabriel Di Bella and Andy Wolfe

An Overview of Cuba's Economy in the 2000s: Recuperation and/or Relapse.
2003, Archibald Ritter

Cuba: An Overview Of Foreign Direct Investment
2002, Dr. Omar Everleny Pérez Villanueva

Does Trade Cause Growth?
1999, Jeffrey Frankel and David Romer

Resources, Agriculture, and Economic Growth in Economies in Transition
2000, Thorvaldur Gylfason

Has The US Embargo Affected The Standard Of Living Of The Cuban People?
2001, Elisa Moncarz, Antonio Jorge and Raul Moncarz

Macroeconomic Policy, Poverty, And Equality In Latin America And The Caribbean
1998, Enrique and Lance Taylor

Growth And Technological Change In Cuba
1997, Manuel Madrid-Aris

What If Cuban Trade Was Based On Economic Fundamentals Instead Of Political Policies? An Estimate Of Cuba's Trade Distortion
2007, Matthew McPherson and William N. Trumbull

Agriculture In The U.S. International Trade Commission Report
2001, William A. Messina, Jr.

Cuba's New Relationship With Foreign Capital: Economic Policy-Making Since 1990
2008, Emily Morris

Has Cuba Definitely Found The Path To Economic Growth?
2000, Roberto Orro

The Cuban Economy In An Unending Special Period
2002, J. F. Pérez-López

The Cuban Economy In Mid-1997
1997, J. F. Pérez-López

Cuban-Soviet Sugar Trade, 1960-1976: How Great Was The Subsidy?
1983, Willard Radell Jr.

Castro's Choices: The Economics of Economic Sanctions
2002, Gary Schiffman

Cuba: Economic Performance Assessment
2009, Nathan Associates Inc.
Economic Sanctions: Effectiveness As Tools Of Foreign Policy.
1992, US General Accounting Office.

Books

The Cuban Economy
(Archibald Ritter)

Cuba: Confronting the US Embargo
(Peter Schwab)

Cuban Communism, 1959-2003
(Eds. Irving Louis Horowitz, Jaime Suchlicki)

Cuba in the World
(Eds. Cole Blasier, Carmelo Mesa-Lago)

Measuring Cuban Economic Performance
(J. F. Pérez-López)

The Cuban Economy: Measurement and Analysis of Socialist Performance
(Andrew Zimbalist and Claes Brundenius)

Failed Sanctions: Why the US Embargo Against Cuba Could Never Work
(Paolo Spadoni)

Cuba (Emily Morris)

Authors, Professors, Economists

Philip Brenner
Claes Brundenius
Eliana Cardoso
Irving Louis Horowitz
Antonio Jorge
Susan Kauffman Purcell
Brian Latell
Carmelo Mesa-Lago
Emily Morris
J. F. Pérez-López
Archibald Ritter
Yoani Sánchez
Peter Schwab
Jaime Suchlicki
Andrew Zimbalist

Appendix 4: Glossary

ALBA - Bolivarian Alliance for the Peoples of Our America; an economic organisation intended to integrate trade, aid and policy among its members; Venezuela, Bolivia, Cuba, Ecuador, Nicaragua, Antigua-Barbuda, Dominica, St. Vincent-Grenadines. It was originally implemented as a trading agreement between Venezuela and Cuba to exchange oil for doctors and teachers.

CARICOM - Caribbean Community; in effect, an economic organisation of French and English speaking countries in the region (i.e. not members of MERCOSUR or ALBA)

ECLAC - UN Economic Commission for Latin America and the Caribbean (CEPAL in Spanish)

Gravity Theory - A theory of international trade that explains trade flows by the distance between the countries and their relative size (GDP). Although distance is still thought to be an important physical factor, it has come to be a catch-all for any factor that impedes trade such as tariffs, language difference, consumer preference, and so on.
See especially J.E. Anderson.

Latin America - an informal term that categorises Spanish and Portuguese speaking nations in Central

America, South America and the Caribbean. The vast majority of continental countries in the region are Latin American, the exceptions being the Guianas and Belize. In contrast, the vast majority in the Caribbean are not Latin American. The exceptions here are Cuba and Dominican Republic, while Puerto Rico is a US possession. Note that these Spanish speaking countries form the majority of the Caribbean's population and economy.

MERCOSUR - Southern Common Market comprised of Argentina, Brazil, Paraguay and Uruguay. The organisation deals with trade, customs, tariffs, sectoral policy etc.

SOUTHERN CONE - an informal geographic descriptor including Argentina, Uruguay and Chile (some consider Paraguay to be included).

ENDNOTES

[1] Report on UN Resolution 63/7. http://embacuba.cubaminrex.cu/Default.aspx?tabid=11014, accessed Sept 20, 2010.

[2] For example, see the UN's Department of Public Information press release: http://www.un.org/News/Press/docs//2008/ga10772.doc.htm

[3] http://www.treasury.gov/resource-center/sanctions/Documents/cda.pdf

[4] www.cubavsbloqueo.cu/Default.aspx?tabid=748

[5]

http://history.state.gov/historicaldocuments/frus1958-60v06/d409

[6] E. Cardoso and A. Helwege; *Cuba After Communism*, MIT Press, 1992, pp 13, 104.

[7] C. Mesa-Lago; *The Economy of Socialist Cuba*, University of New Mexico Press, 1981, p34.

[8] Ibid. p125.

[9] http://www.usitc.gov/publications/docs/pubs/332/pub3398.pdf p 3-34, accessed September 8, 2010.

[10] Ibid. p xiv.

[11] *The need to bring an end to the economic, trade and*

financial blockade imposed by the government of the United States of America against Cuba. Reported in Cuba's Granma Internacional (Digital) October 3 2006.
http://www.granma.cu/ingles/2006/octubre/mar3/41blockade-i.html accessed June 28 2010.
Also see UN 2006 Preliminary Overview of the Economies of Latin America and the Caribbean, p 115.

[12] For example, Report by Cuba on Resolution 59/11 of the United Nations General Assembly, Aug. 15 2005.

[13] All UN references herein are derived from the UN National Accounts Main Aggregates Database, http://unstats.un.org/unsd/snaama/dnlList.asp
[14] US Committee on Foreign Relations: *Legislation on Foreign Relations Through 2002, VOLUME 1-A*; U.S. Government Printing Office, Washington, 2003; p298

[15] *Report by Cuba on Resolution 59/11 of the United Nations General Assembly*; August 15, 2005 (p4)

[16] All Angus Maddison references herein are derived from A. Maddison; *Historical Statistics of the World Economy: 1-2008 AD*. University of Groningen, Groningen Growth and Development Centre (Netherlands)
http://www.ggdc.net/MADDISON/oriindex.htm

[17] J. F. Pérez-López; *Sugar and Structural Change in the Cuban Economy*, World Development, Vol. 17, No. 10, 1989 pp 1629, 1641.

[18] Institute for the Integration of Latin America and the Caribbean; *Integration & Trade*, No. 15 Vol. 5, 2001, pp 41, 47.

[19] Ibid.

[20] P. Lundborg; *The Economics of export embargoes: the case of the US-Soviet grain suspension*; Croom Helm Ltd., Beckenham, 1987, pp 1, 9.

[21] The Caribbean sample includes most of the larger island economies, and is based strictly on the UN's inclusion in its national accounts database. These are: Anguilla, Antigua and Barbuda, Aruba, Bahamas, Barbados, British Virgin Islands, Cayman Islands, Cuba, Dominican Republic, Dominica, Grenada, Haiti, Jamaica, Montserrat, Netherlands Antilles, St. Kitts and Nevis, St. Lucia, St Vincent and the Grenadines, Trinidad and Tobago, Turks and Caicos.

The UN's Latin American list includes:
Argentina, Bolivia, brazil, Chile, Colombia, Costa Rica, Cuba, Dominican Republic, Ecuador, El Salvador, Guatemala, Honduras, Mexico, Nicaragua, Panama, Paraguay, Peru, Uruguay, The Bolivarian Republic of Venezuela.

The GDP per capita values used in this ranking are based on 2005 data to avoid the influence of the current recession.

[22] Maddison; 1950 - Cuba $2,046; small Latin American $1750; small Caribbean $2,533.

[23] J. De Gregorio; *Economic Growth in Latin America: From the Disappointment of the Twentieth Century to the Challenges of the Twenty-First*, Central Bank of Chile Working Papers, No 377 (abstract), Nov. 2006.

[24] *Report by Cuba on Resolution 58/7 of the United Nations General Assembly: "The necessity of ending the economic, commercial and financial blockade imposed by the United States of America against*

Cuba"
Ministerio de Relaciones Exteriores (MINREX). Havana, September 30, 2004.
http://www.cubasource.org/listings/102_e.asp accessed June 29 2010.

[25] US Census Bureau
http://www.census.gov/foreign-trade/balance/

[26] UN Economic Commission for Latin America and the Caribbean (ECLAC); *Latin America and Caribbean in the World Economy 2005-2006*, United Nations Publications, Santiago, 2006, p 27.

[27] Nautical miles from the capital, largest or nearest sea port to Miami. Landlocked Bolivia uses Chile's port distance. Mexico uses roadway distance from Mexico City to Dallas.

[28] Institute for the Integration of Latin America and the Caribbean; *Integration & Trade*, No. 15 Vol. 5, 2001, pp 46, 47.

[29] Ibid.

[30]

www.one.cu/publicaciones/07cuentasnacionales/num indexportac1996-2005/numindexportac1996-2006.pdf

[31] *Report by Cuba on Resolution 59/11 of the United Nations General Assembly*, August 15, 2005 (p4)

[32] I. Horowitz (ed.); *Cuban Communism*, 6th ed., 1987, Transaction Inc., New Brunswick, New Jersey, p 169.

[33] www.cubavsbloqueo.cu/Default.aspx?tabid=283 (last accessed May 9, 2012)

[34] Australia Department of Foreign Affairs and Trade www.dfat.gov.au/publications/tgs/index.html (last accessed April 9, 2012)

[35] For a detailed treatment of persistence, see D. Campbell; *History, Culture, and Trade; A Dynamic Gravity Approach*, UC Davis Working Paper, 2010

[36] Canada's originating legislation was the 1985 Foreign Extraterritorial Measures Act. http://laws-lois.justice.gc.ca/eng/acts/F-29/FullText.html

A related order was issued under the Act in 1992 to address the US Torricelli Act. http://laws-lois.justice.gc.ca/eng/regulations/SOR-92-584/FullText.html
A further amendment was issued in 1996 to address the Helms-Burton Act (see the 1985 Act above).

[37]

http://hdrstats.undp.org/images/explanations/CUB.pdf
http://hdrstats.undp.org/images/explanations/DOM.pdf
also see:
http://hdr.undp.org/en/media/HDR_2011_EN_Table2.pdf

[38] G.C. Hufbauer et al.; *Economic Sanctions Reconsidered: History and Current Policy*, Peterson Institute for International Economics, 1990.

[39] P. Lundborg; ibid., p6.

[40] United States General Accounting Office, National Security and International Affairs Division; *Economic Sanctions: Effectiveness as Tools of Foreign Policy*, Feb. 19, 1992, p2-3.

[41] J. F. Pérez-López; ibid.

www.ingramcontent.com/pod-product-compliance
Lightning Source LLC
Chambersburg PA
CBHW030752180526
45163CB00003B/987